A Day in a Medieval City

By CHIARA FRUGONI

with an introduction by ARSENIO FRUGONI
Translated by WILLIAM MCCUAIG

A DAY IN

A Medieval City

The University of Chicago Press   *Chicago & London*

CHIARA FRUGONI is emerita professor of medieval history at the University of Rome II. Her books include *Francesco e l'invenzione delle stimmate* (Turin, 1993), which won the Viareggio Prize for Nonfiction, 1994; *Vita di un uomo: Francesco d'Assisi* (Turin, 1995); and the *Dizionario del Medioevo*, coedited with A. Barbero (Rome: Laterza, 1994).

ARSENIO FRUGONI (1914–1970) was professor of medieval history at the University of Rome.

WILLIAM McCUAIG is a translator living in Toronto.

The University of Chicago Press, Chicago 60637
The University of Chicago Press, Ltd., London
© 2005 by The University of Chicago
All rights reserved. Published 2005
Paperback edition 2006
Printed in China

14 13 12 11 10 09 08 07 06   3 4 5
ISBN: 0-226-26634-6 (cloth)
ISBN-13: 978-0-226-26635-0 (paper)
ISBN-10: 0-226-26635-4 (paper)

© 1997 by Givs. Laterza & Figli Spa, Roma-Bari. English-language edition arranged through the mediation of Eulama Literary Agency.

Library of Congress Cataloging-in-Publication Data

Frugoni, Chiara, 1940–
     [Storia di un giorno in una citta medievale. English]
     A day in a medieval city / by Chiara Frugoni; with an introduction by Arsenio Frugoni; translated by William McCuaig.
          p. cm.
     Authorship of original Italian edition attributed to Arsenio and Chiara Frugoni; English translation clarifies Arsenio Frugoni's lesser contribution to the current work, which Chiara Frugoni expanded considerably.
     Includes bibliographical references and index.
     ISBN 0-226-26634-6 (cloth: alk. paper)
     1. Cities and towns, Medieval. 2. City and town life—Europe—History. I. Frugoni, Arsenio. II. Title. D134.F7913 2005.
     940.1—dc22
                                                                                           2004025903
This book is printed on acid-free paper.

To my father, now that the span of my years has surpassed that allotted to him

Un fanciullo correva dietro un treno.
La vita—mi gridava—è senza freno.
Salutavo, ridendo, con la mano
e calmo trasalivo, indi lontano.

Sandro Penna

Contents

My father, Arsenio Frugoni, died in 1970 (together with my brother Giovanni) in an automobile accident. He was fifty-six years old. Among his publications was an article marked by his own particular lucid and lively style, recounting the "story of a day in a medieval city" ("Storia di un giorno in una città medievale," *Humanitas* 8 [1953]: 685–693). It appeared without notes, and was in any case too brief to be republished separately. In a work on the history of the city in Italy (*Storia della città in Italia* [Rome: R. A. I., 1956], pp. 43–51), my father returned to this topic, adding a few further, and very charming, pages to what he had already written in his article.

It was my idea to fuse these two pieces into a single composition, add notes to it, and make it the introduction to this book, which I have dedicated to him. The seven chapters I have written all amplify and expand upon my father's short text.

Chiara Frugoni

The translation was made in close collaboration with the author, but I take final responsibility for the English text. In reviewing the Italian original published by Laterza in 1997, she and I have naturally made some corrections and modifications: I have slightly expanded the text in a few places in order to make her point clearer to an English-language readership, and she has updated the bibliographical references and other information given in several footnotes. The title used in English, *A Day in a Medieval City*, is not a literal translation of the original title, *Storia di un giorno in una città medievale*, but readers will find that this book does indeed present the "story" of a day and also a "history" of daily life in a medieval city, or, as she calls it at one point, a ramble through the streets and into the houses and lives of the people of the Middle Ages.

In naming the saints of the Roman Catholic Church I sought no consistency, so some are named in English and others in Italian or Latin, according to whatever seemed most appropriate and familiar in each case. The author normally cites modern scholarly works originally published in English, French, and other languages in their Italian translations if they have been translated into Italian, but I have tried to supply references to the original editions and to English translations of modern works from any language where I could discover that one existed.

For biblical passages, my translation is taken from *The Jerusalem Bible: Reader's Edition* (New York: Doubleday, 1971). But where necessary the English translation is modified to make it conform to the only text of the Bible known to the Middle Ages, and therefore the only one the author cites, the Latin Vulgate. The Vulgate varies from other traditions in the numbering of the poems in the Book of Psalms, so I give references to both systems of numbering.

All translations from medieval sources are my own unless a published translation is explicitly identified in the notes. The book most frequently quoted is Giovanni Boccaccio's collection of novellas or tales, the *Decameron*, a masterpiece of European literature written in the middle of the fourteenth century and cited by the author from the 1993 edition of the critical text first established by Vittore Branca in 1975. I have used, and sometimes adapted, the 1982 English translation of Mark Musa and Peter Bondanella, which is based on the Branca text.

I am grateful to the anonymous reader for the Press who gave an earlier draft of this translation a rigorous critique, and to Maia M. Rigas, the equally rigorous manuscript editor. When I read the proofs in November 2004, I was a fellow at the Italian Academy for Advanced Studies in America at Columbia University, where I had the advantage of being able to discuss points of difficulty with the other fellows. My thanks go to all of them, and to the director of the Academy, David Freedberg.

INTRODUCTION

By Arsenio Frugoni (1914–1970)

The Middle Ages make up about ten centuries of European history. Let us try to pick one moment, an average day somewhere past the middle of this period—say, in the late eleventh or early twelfth centuries, with an occasional glance ahead or behind—when certain ways of living have spread widely, becoming settled and typical, and let us visit one of those cities packed full of houses that are so easy to find in Italy to see what goes on in the course of the day.

The city, that marvelous discovery of the medieval renascence after the year 1000! How many cities had perished prior to that point, in the dreadful desolation that epidemics, invasions, raids, and hunger had caused in the last days of the Roman Empire! It is chilling to think of empty houses dying by degrees, not in a violent drama of fiery destruction and enemy attack, but slowly, as vegetation overpowers everything, penetrating and breaking down and leveling inexorably, with a tempo beyond any human measure.

The men and women (those who were left alive) had for the most part gathered in the shelter of a castle or an abbey that was often virtually a castle as well. There they lived in misery, constrained and deprived of human interaction, hoping that by binding themselves to a powerful and prestigious lord they could survive famine and the assault of predatory barbarians and bandits.

But then things gradually began to settle down in devastated Europe. The blast of warfare grew less frequent. New technical discoveries in the areas of agriculture and transport, the most important of which made the horse into a primitive tractor by harnessing the power of its muscular chest and shoeing its hooves with iron to give them a better grip, made people more secure, setting them free from the tragic and frequent visitation of famine that previous generations had known. The dynamic of a society composed of masters and serfs also changed as the burden of fatiguing work, which was in itself a decisive reason for serfdom, was lifted. And the result of all this was an extraordinary demographic upsurge. New forces were in ferment everywhere around the year 1000. Forests were being cut down and fields cleared: new fields for new men who bore a new relationship to lords who were themselves evolving. Commerce, too, was assuming its enduring features.

The artisans had more work to do to respond to the needs of the growing population. Clusters of houses called *burgi* in Latin and *borghi* in Italian were built outside the city walls, inhabited by enterprising *burgenses* (*borghesi,* or as English speakers say, using the French form of the word, *bourgeois*) who stimulated the production of the goods they needed to buy and sell. Inside the city walls many open fields still remained, but they were being filled up with new houses, and new larger circuits of wall were being built as the expanding city absorbed the bustling *borghi.*

And new cities were rising up around important nodes in the network of communication like abbeys, castles, and sanctuaries. As the numbers of houses surrounding them grew, these nodes soon became cities themselves ringed by their own walls. The walls were certainly a defensive military measure, but they also gave birth to a collective sentiment, as Lewis Mumford rightly pointed out: the walls placed a person either inside or outside the city and determined who did and did not belong. When the gates of the city were shut up at sunset, the city was isolated from the outside world.[1] The walls helped to create a sense of unity among the inhabitants, as though they were together aboard a ship, and in time of siege or famine a moral climate like that on board a ship in peril could easily emerge. Yet inside the walls the "privileged" citizens were not always at peace with one another. The houses of the nobles and the rich sent towers shooting up into the sky above the roofs of the town. The craft guilds proudly displayed their own corporate headquarters and their own churches. There were frequent struggles between factions, each bent on conquering the other, with the loser being driven from the fold, banished from the city.

Yet what a flourishing form of life the cities were, bursting with pride at their own liberty! As they rapidly turned into self-governing communes they defended that liberty through the participation in political life of all the citizens, as in the cities of ancient Greece. The medieval city is truly the symbol of a great epoch in Italian history: the maritime cities of Venice, Genoa, and Pisa dominated Mediterranean commerce with their ships and were soon enriched by far-flung commercial colonies and possessions. Other major cities boasted thriving wool, silk, and arms industries and powerful banks (the Peruzzi bank, for example, was owed fabulous sums by the courts of Europe). Many smaller cities abounded in splendid works of art.

There are characteristic features of the medieval urban fabric that can be seen even today in numerous Italian towns. These commonalities exist even though every one of those towns had a distinct individuality and consequently was a unique entity. The cliché Italian city of the Middle Ages would include a circle of walls pressing tightly against small houses made of dark stone, jammed together and overshadowed by towers made of the same dark stone and laid out with whimsical disorder along tortuous narrow streets. In a word: picturesque. We can start by correcting a few things: the houses certainly did not present so dark a hue then, for their blackness is only the result of oxidation over the course of time. Nor were they so crowded right from the start: often they got that way only in the late Middle Ages, when the vitality that had once driven the cities to expand their circle of walls (some cities rebuilt this costly ring as many as three times because of population growth) was exhausted, and the inhabitants preferred to use ground inside the walls previously occupied by gardens and courtyards to build new houses on. The irregularity of the street plan was sometimes forced upon the builders by the unevenness of the terrain, but it could also be a deliberate artifice to break the force of the winter wind and to give shelter from the summer sun. This point deserves to be emphasized, for we mustn't forget the importance of such physical protection from the extremes of weather, given that the displays and stalls of the artisans and merchants were not protected by windows until at least the seventeenth century and that the greater part of the active life of the citizens took place in the open. Narrow, closed streets and shops that were open to the elements went together: only when the shops were glassed in did new ideas about urban design and wider streets become practicable.[2]

Another cause of the irregular street plan in some cases was an obstruction that has since vanished, like a stream that was later covered over, or a grove of trees that was cut down, or a garden or courtyard later filled in with houses. So is that picturesque disorder an illusion? Is there really an authentic medieval science of urban design? Yes, of course—provided that certain factors are borne in mind.

The ancient city of the type founded by the Romans had shrunk in the early Middle Ages to occupy no more than a small portion of the area enclosed by the ancient ring of walls. Then came the time of resurgence, and the city was rebuilt following the checkerboard pattern of the Roman city in every direction until it came up against the ring of the ancient walls once again. Beyond them roadways and pathways radiated from the city gates into the countryside. Now, when the clusters of houses that had sprung up outside the old walls along these radial roads were encircled in turn by new walls, a curious plan resulted, as the Roman checkerboard and the fanlike pattern of roadways meshed with one another. Bologna is an example, where the two poles of the ancient *decumanus* form a contrast to a spiderweb of what were once country roads. But in new cities that grew up along major arteries of communication, a geometric plan might also come into being, as houses were laid out in a herringbone pattern and streets running parallel to the main one were added to produce something very like the Roman checkerboard.

Most typically, however, the medieval city was radial in form. Construction and development wrapped themselves around an abbey, a castle, or an open space used as a market, a process often favored by the elevated position of the core that had served to generate it. In order to explain this typically radial medieval plan, scholars have invoked the influence of the circular encampments and villages of the barbarian peoples; or they have invoked the influence of the Eastern peoples, contact with whom was promoted by the Crusades. But maybe the radial plan was simply a natural expression of vigorous growth around a central nucleus, of an organic subordination of the spreading city to the core that gave it life, which the geometric checkerboard plan, every allotment identical and interchangeable with every other, could certainly never fulfill. And for that matter, even when it was not radial, the plan of the medieval city expressed a will to insert oneself into an environment and exploit it, not to build according to a drearily geometric layout. Hence, even when the city was virtually a checkerboard, having arisen along a road, the allotments were not regular, and in this way the linearity of the streets was shattered; if laid out at a bend in a river, they slanted as they followed its curve.

The Middle Ages were not egalitarian, but fundamentally hierarchical. Hierarchy meant the individuation of one's dignity, of one's responsibility, and this individuation was strongly expressed in the city. Specialization determined the physiognomy of the streets and neighborhoods. Ethnic specialization appeared in the ghetto, where the Jews lived out of a desire to preserve their characteristic way of life and because the majority found the mixture of religions troubling. But it was optional— the obligation to reside in a closed quarter bounded by walls and gates was first imposed in Turin in the fifteenth century. There were streets inhabited by close-knit communities of foreigners where they pursued their trades and activities. There was professional specialization, with streets inhabited entirely by artisans engaged in a particular craft. A few surviving street names still refer to this: via degli Orefici (street of the goldsmiths), via dei Calderari (street of the coppersmiths), via dei Funari (street of the ropemakers), via dei Mercanti (street of the merchants), and via dei Patari (street of rag-dealers[3]) still speak to us of those former specializations. There were residential quarters too, without shops, cut off from traffic and the clamor of urban life.

In the piazza, the characteristic yet miraculous creation of the Middle Ages, the spirit of distinct specialization also held sway. The medieval city had three kinds of piazza, usually separate from one another: the religious piazza, the political piazza, and the economic piazza. The religious piazza was the piazza of the cathedral: one of its characteristics was its modest size, but the buildings surrounding it were low, so that the church stood out in contrast. And it was a piazza into which high streets full of traffic never triumphantly disgorged—either the streets ran past it, or if they did lead directly into it, they never did so at a right angle. Often it was flanked by further narrow piazzas that isolated it even more. Examples of this way of organizing public space are common in the cities of Umbria, Lazio, Tuscany, and Lombardy, at any rate where iconoclastic modern urban planners have not thought it their duty to clear it away in order to create one immense piazza, like the Piazza del Duomo in Milan. In the piazza of the cathedral were performed the sacred pageants, and it was there that the processions took place, with the people participating,—actors more than spectators, or at least, spectators with a role to play in the spectacle, observing it from inside rather than outside, as the images from that distant world show us. From the height of the bell tower, the church bells summoned the other bells of the city to synchronize the work, the prayers, and the repose of the people.

The political piazza normally had larger dimensions, since it was intended for gatherings of the entire citizenry. In cities with a radial plan, it was the heart of the city, but even in this case the streets did not funnel all the traffic onto the piazza but instead ran past it. Tightly ringed and dominated by the *palazzo pubblico* (city hall would be the English equivalent), it was often adorned with a decorative fountain, or with an *arengo,* a rostrum or dais from which speeches were made, or with columns bearing the symbols of power or banners displaying standards.

The economic piazza, the marketplace, was generally located close by the political piazza to which it was joined by short passageways, or *piazzette.* In cities that grew out of Roman foundations it normally appeared at the interface between the ancient and the medieval parts of the city. In cities that grew up around an abbey or a castle, however, the market piazza appeared directly in front of the institution that had formed the nucleus. Sometimes the market was spread out over several piazzas specializing in different types of merchandise: the fish market, the vegetable market, the meat market. Fountains for washing the vegetables, stone basins for meat and fish, or arcades that virtually created a covered marketplace—even today these features still bear witness to the great care devoted to this aspect of city life at a time when everything was brought together every day in the one central location where people went to get their foodstuffs instead of shopping as they do today, in specialty stores dispersed throughout town. Despite modern urban redevelopment, it is still easy to find wonderful examples of the three typical kinds of medieval piazza even today.

Now let us choose a city at random and set off down one of the streets. If our city was built on uneven terrain there will often be a series of steps to make the ascent easier and keep the roadbed in place, for by no means were all streets paved; only in 1235 was paving provided for pedestrians in Florence. But the streets are always narrow and tortuous anyway, made jagged by houses that unexpectedly protrude, so that we immediately wonder how carts and wagons managed to circulate. The fact is that the street in a medieval city was more a line of communication for individuals moving about on foot as they attended to their needs and their business than it was a route for transportation. Rows of porticos offered shelter from the rain, as did, failing all else, the markedly overhanging roofs of the houses. As in the rest of the Mediterranean world, the roofs are hardly slanted at all; umbrellas only appeared in Italy in the sixteenth century. The narrowness and tortuousness of the streets help to protect pedestrians from the sun and the wind. But for the darkness of nighttime there is no remedy: no illumination is provided except for the flickering light of candles placed before holy images (so their function is not purely devotional), and rather than illuminate they serve at best to guide the few passersby who are forced to venture out at night in the deserted city.

By day, though, the street is full of life. Artisans display their wares there, and do their work when necessary; and there, by scrutinizing the goods for sale, one sharpens one's eye for detail and one's taste. Chickens and even pigs frequently roam in the streets, just as they would in a farmyard, and the job of disposing of the city's garbage is left to them (or to the rainwater). Are the streets filthy? Everyone makes it their own personal business to keep the street clean in front of their own house— a system still used today in small towns, and sometimes in the cities for clearing snow from the sidewalks.

All the citizens are like members of one big family, and they get to know one another as they make their way through the domestic streets. Suddenly we emerge into an open space, or a piazza, and find a public well. While the women wait their turn at the well they exchange a wealth of news about what is going on in the city and they carry it back home with them, along with the water.

The medieval city, after the eleventh century, had so much fervent life and confidence that we can readily recognize characteristics of our own modern world in it. But it is also extraordinarily different in many ways, and we need to emphasize that as well as we follow medieval people through an average day. Between the evening twilight and the grayness before dawn, one can hardly even make out the walls of the houses, for there is no lighting in the medieval city, as we said. At evening curfew the women cover the coals in the hearth with ash to reduce the fire hazard and keep them alive until next morning. The houses are built with beams of oak and every one is a potential tinderbox waiting to blaze up, so at night the only flames left burning are the candles before the holy images. Why would the streets need to be lit anyway? In the evening the entrances to the dangerous neighborhoods are barred, chains are stretched across the river to prevent a surprise attack from barbarian raiders coming upstream, and the city gates are locked tight. The city is like one big household, with everything well secured.

Undeniably picturesque by day, the streets seem even more narrow and twisting by night. They are made that way because of the pressure of the walls, thick and high, and reinforced with gates as robust as castles that cannot easily be expanded because of the cost. If the population inside grows rapidly, then the houses get jammed together haphazardly, new ones clinging to old, as the builders fit them in as best they can. And old buildings are never cleared away to make a fresh start, unless fire or factional violence intervene to do the job.

The houses are small. The ground floor consists of a long room, with a shop at the front if the inhabitant is an artisan, and a kitchen and eating area at the rear, so that even when gathered around the large fire, to cook or just to keep warm, the family can still keep an eye on the shop. Working life and domestic life are closely interwoven, so that those who work in the boss's house eat together at the same table, work in the same room, sleep in the same sleeping quarters, take part in family prayers together, and share the same common amusements. This absence of differentiated space and functions was a notable feature of the medieval house. (Even in the bedroom, on the upper floor of the house, there was no intimacy except perhaps in the most lordly households; desire for that kind of intimacy only developed slowly, and in the seventeenth century the maids still slept on cots at the foot of their masters' beds, and a room in an inn might offer its hospitality to half a dozen strangers at a time.)

Sometimes, though, the dining room, which is reached by a small outside staircase, occupies the second floor, and from there an internal staircase leads to the rooms on the third. Bodily functions are accommodated in many houses by a small protruding hutch with a seat that opens directly into a canal, or if there is no canal, into a pit kept well covered with ash, or into a large tub. Alternatively, they use chamber pots and empty the contents into the street. The rain washes a lot of it away, and during the daytime of course the hens and dogs and pigs are there to clean up the streets. For the rest, everyone takes care of cleaning up the street directly in front of their own house—on important feast days anyway, when everything is scrubbed and the facades of all the houses are hung with beautiful cloths.

Inside the houses the furniture is solid, the massive planks generously cut to make them sound and robust. The essential pieces of furniture are the bed and a long low chest. The chest holds clothing (which is normally rolled up tightly when it is put away), underwear perfumed with sweet-smelling herbs, the important family documents on parchment, and money in a leather purse. But the money, and the jewels if there are any, are more often kept in a casket, bound with iron and carefully locked, under the bed. The bed itself can be amazingly large, for not uncommonly half a dozen people might be sleeping in it. A straw mattress and feather pillows make it soft. For the poor, however, bed is a box filled with hay and a pillow stuffed with straw. And inside the houses bales of straw often take the place of seats and benches, and naturally if one wants to pretty the place up or honor a special guest, they can be draped with textiles. Such a seat is especially welcome in cold weather.

Now let us try to bring this city of houses to life.

The peal of a bell rings through the air and other bells respond to it, muffled by distance. It is the start of another day, a day that still takes its rhythm from the bells that set the pace of monastic life: matins at midnight, and then, at intervals of three hours, lauds, prime, terce, sext (rung at midday, whence the expression "to take a siesta"), and then nones, vespers, and compline. At intervals of three hours, we said, but note that in the Middle Ages three hours did not constitute a uniform period. The fact is that the twelve hours of the night and the twelve hours of the day did not always last the same length of time, for they were not counted off by mechanical instruments. Instead, day and night were divided into twelve segments that grew longer and shorter as day and night themselves grew longer and shorter during the course of the year. The result was that in summer, for example, one hour of daylight lasted a lot longer than an hour of daylight in the winter. An anecdote supplied from a chronicle by the great medievalist Marc Bloch illustrates wonderfully well this species of perpetual ebb and flow of time:

> At Mons a judicial duel was supposed to take place. But at dawn only one of the antagonists showed up; and at the ninth hour, which was the end of the waiting period prescribed by custom, he asked that the failure of his adversary to appear be officially recorded. Juridically speaking he was clearly within his rights. But had the prescribed hour really passed? The county judges deliberated; they looked at the sun; they requested an opinion from the clerics, on whom the performance of the liturgy had imprinted a close acquaintance with the rhythm of the hours and who made use of the church bells to sound their beat, more or less accurately, for the benefit of the whole community. Clearly, the court pronounced, the ninth hour had passed. How distant that society, in which a tribunal had to debate and take expert advice in order to establish what time it was, appears from our civilization, and from us ourselves, accustomed as we are to live with one eye constantly fixed on the clock![4]

People get up tremendously early in the Middle Ages. The lazy lie-a-bed students who choose to sign up for the course on Gratian's *Decretum* are talked about in scandalized tones because the lectures take place at the third hour—which is only about 9:00 A.M., after all, when most industrious employees in our time begin their working day without feeling guilty. Everyone else gets up a lot earlier than that. They make a triple sign of the cross in honor of the Holy Trinity and then get completely dressed. Fashion was changeable even then, so we can skip a detailed description of what they wore, but it is worth mentioning that artifice and sacrifice were accepted then as now by women worried about their appearance, who used an endless array of hair colorants, cosmetics, depilatories, lotions, and perfumes.

Only after they are completely dressed do they wash their hands and faces, the sole parts of the body left uncovered. This regimen is dictated by the absence of a room for washing and dressing separate from the bedroom, which is always overpopulated anyway. But don't they ever take a bath? Certainly: after a long voyage, for example, or if they have gotten particularly dirty for some reason. Then they use the laundry tub. But there are also public baths with hot water. In the morning, as soon as the water is good and hot, criers set out through the streets to let the whole town know. In Paris in 1292 there were twenty-six public baths for 200,000 inhabitants, open every day except feast days. Nevertheless, nobody could say that people in the Middle Ages were exactly squeaky clean.

The sun has not yet risen when people leave the house to go to church. Everyone who is physically able and can find the time attends mass. Medieval people were believers par excellence. The vision of mankind's destiny and that of the universe offered by Christianity had a place for all of them. People in the Middle Ages did not think of the supernatural as something apart from earthly life here below. Today we see earthly life as running its own course, satisfying interests that contain their own self-justification, while the supernatural concerns life after death, something we worry about so as not to prejudice our fate in the long future of eternity. The Middle Ages were different, for then the supernatural and the earthly interpenetrated one another. In fact, to those able to reflect upon the matter, the sensible world appeared to be no more than a kind of mask, with all the really important things taking place on the other side. Or else events that take place here were merely signs of a more profound reality. Medieval man thus felt that nature was no more than a crust beneath which divine powers were in motion, and that in history he was only playing a part alongside other invisible and very important actors. "Who doesn't realize," writes the priest Helmhold, "that wars, hurricanes, plagues, in truth all the evils that befall the human race, come about through the work of demons?"[5] Hence the need to resort to the operation of means more effective than human effort. A pilgrimage was just as valid a way for a king to avert a war as an alliance was. For simple mortals, a mass was just as valid a way to avert an illness or make a business deal turn out well as taking medicine or a trip—more valid, in fact.

Given this typical, vigorously imaginative, medieval mentality—the feeling that there was a sort of physical linkage between the earthly city and the invisible city, with the earthly city inhabited promiscuously by men and angels, demons and saints—it should cause no surprise that a cynical statesman like Rainald of Dassel, the chancellor of Emperor Frederick I Barbarossa, should have been preoccupied with obtaining the relics of the three Wise Men, held in Milan, for his own church. Those relics signified the authentic operative presence of powerful saints: the power of the saint resided in the reliquary, ready to intervene against enemies and demons, who were always naturally in league. And so, given that bold power of the imagination, they could conceive that the operative presence of the saint had weight; indeed, that it was weighable. One thinks of a certain set of linens that were weighed before being lowered through a hole and left all night by the burial place of a martyr, and then in the morning, before being given to a devout pilgrim as a relic, were weighed again to see how much heavier they were—for they were now imbued with grace.[6]

We shouldn't smile at this. The supernatural was a reality and a corporeal reality at that, more true even than natural reality. To give the sense of this reality, in which it was natural for the divine to take part in the affairs of mankind for the purpose of bringing about precise outcomes, we should remember God's judgment, not a miracle but an inevitable and decisive intervention of God himself. So when medieval people paused to contemplate ultimate reality and the meaning of life, they were overwhelmed by their own turbulent religious sentiment—an inner world, distinctively medieval, thronging with angels and demons, and dominated by heaven and hell and, above all, by the Last Judgment: "Dies irae dies illa, solvet saeculum in favilla," the day of wrath, the day the earth will dissolve into flames, as David and the Sibyl said, when there will be trembling, when the Judge will come at last.[7]

When would the Last Judgment arrive? Saint Paul had said it would come by surprise: "the Day of the Lord is going to come like a thief in the night" (1 Thess. 5:2). And the surprise must certainly be near: in war, disorder, and pestilence, the people of the Middle Ages discerned signs that the end of days was approaching. We can truthfully say that the Last Judgment was the obsession of the Middle Ages. But because the obsession was ever-present, it was taken for granted. People reawoke to it when an event or a chronological calculation brought the fatal appointment to mind. It was like death. This doesn't mean that they didn't live their lives to the full. But they did so in bursts, with highs and lows, with an emotionality compounded of fury and desperation, joy and tears (how they cry in the medieval chronicles!) that derives from their complete, undetached involvement in an earthly reality that, like a veil suddenly rent, could show itself to be different, supernatural. You summon a doctor to drive out a disease, but the disease is also the devil. You fight a war to gain something or defend it, but war is also a sign of the end of the world. The well-being that you achieve through your efforts and in which you and your family take delight, might be a sin and a damnation. Hence their disconcerting changeableness: their way of sobbing at a sermon after having bellowed with laughter at table; those kings that alternate betrayal with charity; those unforeseen conversions that come like lightning, with no warning; in sum, that agitated medieval world, where men are capable of unheard-of violence, cruelty, debauchery; and sacrifice, mortification of the flesh, and abstinence. Medieval people had not yet learned to harmonize the conduct of life, to experience faith as the certainty of a future beatitude, different to well-being in this life, which we spend in acting for the good, or simply in acting.

Now mass is over. The working day finally begins, and we are still only at about 6:00 A.M. After early breakfast—there will be another at around 9:00 A.M.—everyone gets busy. The artisans open their shops; the doctors, wearing their characteristic reddish purple caps and red gloves, commence their rounds; the criers are making themselves heard round the wagon of the itinerant haberdasher; the market gardeners head out to the fields; and domestic animals crowd the streets, which suddenly burst into life.

At home the housewife gives orders to her servants and daughters about cooking and laundry, based on what she has been taught and has learned from experience. The wisdom of home remedies! Here is a very practical one: "When covers or furs or clothing infested with fleas are enclosed and sealed up, as in a trunk tightly bound with straps, or in a sack that is squeezed and well tied, or otherwise placed or compressed so that the fleas get no light or air and have no room to move, they will die in a short time."[8] And here is a medicine that never fails if you have been bitten by a rabid dog: "Take a crust of bread and write on it: '+ bestera + bestie + nay + brigonay + dictera + sagragan + es + domina + fiat + fiat + fiat.'"[9]

The children meanwhile are in school, unless they are still young enough to be frolicking at home or in the street or already old enough to be working in a shop. Shall we visit the schoolroom? A delightful textbook written for an episcopal school in question-and-answer form, like a catechism, gives us the chance: miraculously it brings the voices of the master (M.) and the little schoolboy (S.) who has memorized his replies back to life.[10]

M.   *Es tu scholaris?* Are you a schoolboy?

S.   Yes, I am.

M.   What is a schoolboy?

S.   One who is solicitous to learn virtue.

M.   Where are you a schoolboy?

S.   Here, everywhere, and in every honest place.

M.   What are the honest places?

S.   Four: church, school, my parents' house, and the gathering of the wise.

M.   Why are you a schoolboy?

S.   Because I go frequently to school and I learn to read.

M.   How many are the works of a schoolboy?

S.   Six.

M.   What are they?

S.   Get up in the morning, get dressed immediately, comb my hair, wash my hands, praise God, and go willingly to school.

M.   Who made you?

S.   God, out of nothing.

M.   Who begot you?

S.   My mother.

M.   How did she beget you?

S.   I was begotten naked, and in original sin.

But the answers did not always come back as promptly as they do in this textbook, and that was when smacks were liberally dealt out with those damned rods: once, in 937, exasperated schoolboys set fire to the monastery of Saint Gallen, using as kindling the rods that the masters had imprudently sent the boys themselves to bring down from the attic.[11]

But other times the schoolboys were as meek as lambs. The schoolmaster dictated little notions to them like these, which I take from the same textbook: "Reverend master, my parents have sent me to Your Worthiness to beg you to come to dinner with them tomorrow." Or else: "Venerable master, my parents honor you with this small gift, and they offer you this little bottle of wine."[12] The master was a sly fellow, all right! But let us close our notebooks and head for home, because it is time for dinner.

What did they eat in the Middle Ages? Given the difficulty of transportation, it is clear that every area consumed mostly local produce. And certainly the difference between the menu of the upper classes and that of the rest of the population was very much greater than it is today. The impression one gets reading over certain accounts of official dinners is that of an enormous quantity of meat, especially game, all of it seasoned with sauces dense with spices, and accompanied by candied fruit and spicy sweets, with never a lighter dish to give a breather.

And their diet seems even heavier to us when we realize that our forefathers did not use plates or forks or napkins. They used large slices of bread on which they placed the meat and the sauce and ate it like that—with what dainty bites we can well imagine. The slice of bread, or whatever was left of it, they tossed into a container at the center of the table, to be used as alms for the poor. If there was a tablecloth they used it to wipe their fingers, so that it had to be changed several times during the meal, even though they also used water to rinse their mouths and hands. Wine was served with dessert and not before. Naturally ordinary people ate more simply. The basic food every day of the year for the common people was soup, cooked with a piece of smoked pork, except on fast days.

But whether it was smoked pork or spiced game, they certainly ate a lot. In comparison with the tastes of austerely rationed modern people like ourselves, we need only observe the provision specified for those employed in a *corvée* at the Abbey of

Montbourg: it consisted of "a large loaf, bean soup, six eggs, and as much to drink as required." During Lent, as penitence, the eggs were replaced by "three herrings and nuts." After dinner it was time for a siesta. There was banter and joking, for as Boccaccio says, after eating everyone likes to have what he likes best.[13] The artisan emerges from his doorway to chat with his neighbors about this and that.

At such times the taste, typical of the Middle Ages, for laughing long and loud at derisive tricks bordering on cruelty, was likely to explode. I will mention just one story as an example, which must have been greatly appreciated, since it turns up so often. The narrative always goes more or less as follows: a merchant departed for a voyage of two years. When he returned he found that his wretched wife had had a child. The wife, to clear herself, claimed that one day, while in the mountains, she had eaten some snow because she felt thirsty, and that she had gotten pregnant as a result. The merchant bided his time. Five years later he left for another voyage, taking the boy with him, whom he sold into slavery across the sea for one hundred pounds. When he returned, his wife asked him where the lad was and he answered: "The sun was so hot in those parts that he melted away, since he came from the snow."[14] People back then could laugh at this jest, atrociously inhuman for us. Truly, every age has its own sense of humor.

Now evening is falling over the medieval city. There is still some work to finish up, and one more meal to eat, but this one is lighter, for at night the Evil One prowls like a roaring lion, searching for someone to eat.[15] A wonderful little book from those times advises a housewife to avoid eating too much in the evening, free herself from all earthly and mundane thoughts, retire to a solitary place, and think of nothing except that tomorrow, early in the morning, she will go to hear mass and make a "good, mature, measured confession" of her sins.[16]

Apart from a small band of revelers that are making the rounds of the taverns to play at dice, ever on the lookout for a dispute or a jest, the people of the city abandon the streets and get ready for bed as naturally as the hens and the dogs and the pigs seek out their places of shelter at the approach of evening. Clothes are hung on a horizontal pole to protect them from the animals of the house, the dogs or the mice or whatever. But not their shirts. Those are only removed under the bedcovers, for people sleep nude and put their shirts back on first thing in the morning. And so they go to sleep.

At regular intervals during the night the monks will leave their beds to sing matins and lauds for the protection of those who are sleeping. In the serene nighttime sky the stars shine down in their thousands until the roosters crow and it is time to start another ordinary day.

Ey comance le no? liute des
propuetez des choses qui
tuute d n teps z de ses p f
ius que nous auons dit
du ciel z de ses parties

✦ Figure 1. *Agricultural Labor throughout the Year.* Miniature, 1445–1450, from Bartholomeus Anglicus, *On the properties of things* (*De proprietatibus rerum*). Paris, Bibliothèque Nationale, MS Fr. 135, fol. 327.

Chapter One

THE TIME OF LABOR, THE TIME OF MEMORY

In a manuscript (1445–1450)[1] of *De proprietatibus rerum* (On the Properties of Things), an encyclopedic work of the thirteenth century
by Bartholomeus Anglicus, a miniature appears first at the beginning
of book 9, which deals with "Time and Its Parts." Here the author reflects upon the heavens, the solstices and the equinoxes, the sun and
the moon, the dawn and the sunset, the seasons, the months, and the
days. It was a gifted but unknown artist from the north of France who
confronted the difficult task (for he had no established pattern to follow) of devising an effective visual heading for the pages of text laid
out for the reader. Let us watch him at work (fig. 1).

Inside a rectangular gilded frame a vortex of delicate wisps of cloud,
discreetly signifying atmospheric time and its immense rhythms, swirls
about the circle of the Earth, which is visualized in four segments, each
occupied by a peasant intent on seasonal labor in the open fields. At
the center, inside a house of stout timber providentially open to view,
a meditative, well-dressed man (look closely: his robe is lined with fur)
raises his foot before a crackling fire in a mobile four-wheeled brazier.
The artist has portrayed him in a moment of repose, beside a table laid
with a white tablecloth, a pitcher of wine, and a loaf of bread: the sym-
bolic fruits of an entire year of labor.

The four peasants belong to four successive stages of life, shown
clockwise. At the top left the youngest, still almost a child in fact, is
gathering clusters of grapes from vines spread on trellises and placing
them in a basket lying at his feet. The top right depicts a young man
engaged in reaping: the stalks of grain, all of equal height, fall to the

ground before the rhythmic swing of his sickle. An adult man follows in the lower right, mowing the hay in broad swathes, with a hollow horn filled with water hanging from his belt, in which he keeps the whetstone he uses from time to time to sharpen the blade of his scythe. An elderly man comes last, heavily dressed to keep out the biting cold and carrying seeds of wheat in a pouch that he has formed by lifting the front of his apron. He is scattering these in the furrows already traced by the plow.

Our gaze moves clockwise as it follows the stages of life, but if we look counter-clockwise—as the layout of the figures suggests we do—we will perceive a different cycle, that of the seasons, starting with winter: man sows, then mows, then reaps, and at last harvests grapes. The possibility of reading the painting in two contrary directions is an invention of the illuminator, who wanted to emphasize not the passage of time but instead the labor of man over the course of the year. The dominant theme is thus the drudgery of the peasant, whose eyes never meet ours because his back is stooped to the earth, whose every waking moment is dedicated to eking out a living and surviving in obedience to the divine condemnation: "Accursed be the soil by your work. With toil shall you get your food from it all the days of your life."[2]

The perspective is slightly tilted so that instead of earth and sky we see only the earth: fields in bloom, fields turning to green, fields stripped bare. The pale blue sky does, however, transpire through the narrow window of the house where the man sits, finally at ease, sheltered from the vagaries of the weather and from hunger—the pivotal point of all the actions performed by the peasants.

The cyclical repetition of the labor of the fields, of measured efforts that never change, had already been wonderfully rendered in a miniature (datable to 1281–1284 and unfortunately not completed; fig. 2) that illustrates a miracle narrated in one of the *Cantigas de Santa María* (Canticles of Santa Maria) of Alfonso X the Wise.[3] At Easter the monks in an English monastery were together in church, intent on celebrating the mass, when the earth opened without warning, and the monastery and all the fields around it disappeared into a chasm. But the Virgin Mary, to whom the monks were very devoted, protected them: no one was hurt, and life continued underground the way it had on the surface, because "the church, the cloister, the dormitory, the chapter hall, the refectory, the kitchen, the parlor, the infirmary, the cellar with the wine and all the accessories, the kitchen gardens and the mills" were not damaged by their plunge into the deep. When Easter came round again a year later, the monks too "rose" with Christ through the intervention of the Madonna, who caused all the fields and buildings to return to their place "just like that, the way they were before."

The illuminator has divided the page into six panels, to be read from left to right and top to bottom. In the

Figure 2. *The Miracle of the Monastery That Sinks into the Depths of the Earth, Then Reemerges.* Miniature, 1281–1284, from Alfonso X the Wise, *Cantigas de Santa María.* Florence, Biblioteca Nazionale Centrale, MS B. R. 20, fol. 15r.

first are shown the church interior, the officiating priest, and the monks at prayer, and along with them the exterior of the abbey and its outbuildings, a closely planted vineyard, fields, and a handsome water mill. In the second panel the catastrophe is shown by the meadow with red and blue flowers that now surrounds the abbey, even covering the roof so that the spectator will understand that the whole complex has been submerged. The scene in the third panel is very similar to the one before, with the flowered meadow reappearing. But observe the vineyard, now bare of leaves, where a peasant is cutting back the vines: with heaven's permission, everything continues as before beneath the earth, and man contributes his own labor to the course of the seasons. The vines are sending out tender shoots in the fourth panel (by now we understand where we are, and there is no use repeating the flowered meadow), and the monks are beginning to implore the Virgin, who has appeared on the altar with her Child on a golden throne to consummate the miracle. Time passes and we arrive at the fifth panel, where the supplication continues with more urgency and animation, while the vines have already put forth numerous leaves. In the sixth panel the miracle has come about: the monks prostrate themselves in thanks, and the vines are as luxuriant as they were at the outset. The annual religious cycle, unchanged from year to year, coincides with the hard work done by human hands through the endless loop of the seasons. The peasant perseveres in the toil imposed on Adam after the Fall; the agricultural way of life has profound religious value, for the Church portrays it as biblical punishment but equally as the means of redemption. In this canticle it is not an accident, I think, that with the resurrection of Christ, who comes to free Adam and his descendants, both the fields and the men who work them also rise again.

Now let us focus on an image that shows us the seasons from a different point of view, in a miniature that illustrates the chapter concerning them in a manuscript of the *Secretum secretorum* (Secret of Secrets) copied and illuminated around 1490–1495 (fig. 3). The artist has shaped the frame in such a way as to suggest a window opening onto a surprising vista: four strips, vertically stacked, each of them a distant, self-contained landscape. The first of these strips (in descending order) shows us gentle hills through which a river runs, ordered and plentiful fields, a few trees, distant castles against a tranquil sky. This harmonious springtime landscape is followed by that of summer: in the foreground a dense crop of ripe stalks and sheaves already set in rows among the leafy trees. Autumn has come, the third strip says to us: the leaves have fallen, the branches are bare, the shrubbery withered. The bottom landscape belongs to winter, with a sheet of ice instead of open water, the ground now bare and frosty, the trees standing starkly, like black contorted silhouettes. Nature has fallen still and silent, and a few lowering fortresses fit perfectly into the gloomy panorama it presents.

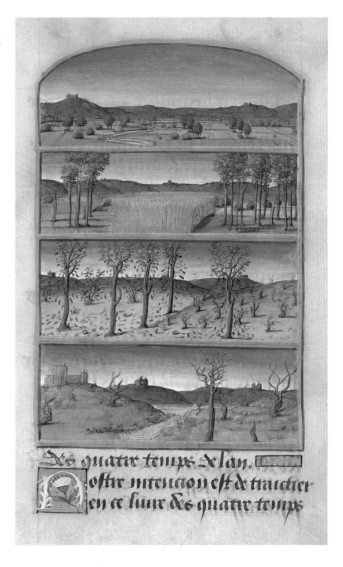

Figure 3. *The Four Seasons*. Miniature, 1490–1495, from Pseudo-Aristotle, *Secretum secretorum*. Paris, Bibliothèque Nationale, MS Nouvelle Acq. Fr. 18145, fol. 50r.

The author of this unusual landscape painting perhaps wished to depict the stages of human life, from the carefree youth of springtime to the melancholy decline of wintertime. There is no sign of any humans or any agricultural activity: space within time holds uncontested sway.[4] Yet, between time as the cyclical representation of human toil, with the peasant bent in submission to nature and its immutable rhythms (as the brilliant illuminator of the *De proprietatibus rerum* conceives it) and the representation of nature as though it were the moving hands of a clock, indifferent to human presence or absence (as with the illuminator of the *Secretum secretorum*) there is a third kind of time, that of the city, a landscape of humans alone.

In the city the background is still religious, and Christmas and Easter and the feast days of the saints do not change, but in the foreground new buildings are rising and old ones are being torn down: things that human beings themselves decide are giving the years their rhythm. Rather than atmospheric time rotating in an endless cycle, unvarying through the succession of the months and the seasons (fig. 3 above) or the labor of the fields that forces man to plod in time's wake as though he were its shadow, trimming the vines in spring each year for all the springs of a lifetime (fig. 2 above), it is the actions of man, and diversified, specialized, innovative work, that forge a different kind of time in the city: the time of memory.

Chapter Two

THE ROAD THAT LEADS TO THE CITY

I n the communal cities of the Middle Ages, the inhabitants were as
proud of the beautiful walls of the city they lived in as they were of
the facades of their own houses. About the Florence of 1324, Giovanni
Villani wrote, "The order was given that a tower 60 braccia in height
and 14 braccia in width should be made every 200 braccia along the
wall, for the strength and the beauty of the city."[1] Dino Compagni felt
sincerely sorry when his fellow Florentines destroyed the walls of Pistoia: "The beautiful walls of the city were torn down."[2] They appreciated the aesthetic merit of the walls, but they also knew how much
their city needed them to survive.[3] Rabanus Maurus conveyed this in
the middle of the ninth century, behind a veil of metaphor, in his *De
Universo*: "The walls of the city signify the invincible firmness of faith,
hope, and charity."[4] Faith, hope, and charity are the theological virtues,
but they functioned as supremely civic virtues during the flowering of
the communes, guaranteeing good government. This is because love of
the city one calls home has its roots in charity, according to the defini-
tion of Ptolemy of Lucca, and the actions of justice are animated by
faith and by hope for divine guidance.[5] These are precisely the virtues
that are balanced around the personage of the *Bene Comune* (The Common Good) in the celebrated fresco by Ambrogio Lorenzetti, known
as *Il Buon Governo* (Good Government), painted in 1338–1339 in the
Sala della Pace (the Room of Peace) in the Palazzo Pubblico of Siena
(fig. 4). The words of Rabanus Maurus can be applied, I think, to the
analysis of a small biccherna panel of 1480 by Neroccio di Bartolom-
meo di Benedetto de' Landi (fig. 5),[6] in which the kneeling Virgin

commends Siena to Jesus. The Madonna draws a cord about an idealized, but easily recognizable, image of Siena with its protective wall of compact bricks. The folk etymology of the word *concordia* ("concord") from "cum chorda" ("with a cord") accounts for the presence of the cord, for it symbolizes the civic unity that the Virgin is intervening to ensure, her direct interest revealed by the words of the scroll she holds in her hand, "This is my city" (*Haec est cívitas mea*). The scaled-down model of Siena in this painting stands ("invincible firmness") on three marble columns of different hue: white, dark green, and dark red, the traditional colors of faith, hope, and charity.[7]

The walls and gates of the city, like the walls and doors of one's own home, give shelter and inspire a feeling of security.[8] To emphasize how Christ shared the lives of the marginalized and the defenseless right from his birth, the Dominican preacher Giordano da Pisa reminded his listeners that Christ was born "in a small and lowly town, *nor was he born inside it, but outside*."[9] And terror is the contrasting emotion that fills whoever chances to find himself shut out of the reassuring refuge: such a disaster can only be redeemed by a miracle, as we see in a story told in another of the canticles (no. 246) of Alfonso X the Wise, which is accompanied, like all those in the manuscript, by a full-page illustration (fig. 6).[10]

A good woman of Alcázar, a devotee of the Virgin, left the city every Saturday and went to the Church of Santa María de los Mártires, where she prayed and left the customary offering. One time she was delayed by household chores and arrived in the evening to find the entrance to the church already closed. As she was regretting her lateness, for which she blamed herself, she realized with amazement that the door had mysteriously opened for her—and after her prayers were finished it closed behind her just as mysteriously as she left. The good woman then set off at a rapid pace to regain the city, but night had already fallen when she reached the walls, and she found the gate barred. What a sense of desolation and fear! There was nothing to do but commend herself to the Virgin. Then a beautiful and noble lady appeared, took her by the hand, and brought her into the city and into her own house. "Who am I, my lady, that you should do such a service for a poor person?" And the lady happily answered, "I am she who comes to give aid when misfortunes occur that require my assistance; I am she whom God chose to incarnate himself." Nor was her assistance out of proportion in this case; it responded to a profound emotion. The Madonna understood the poor woman's anguished fear of the dark, of solitude, above all, of being shut out—not just from her home, but excluded from the city itself.

Figure 4. *Faith, Hope, and Charity Flanking the Common Good*. Ambrogio Lorenzetti, detail from *Good Government* (*Il Buon Governo*), fresco, 1338–1339. Siena, Palazzo Pubblico, Sala della Pace. Scala / Art Resource, NY.

Figure 5. *The Virgin Commends Siena to Jesus*. Neroccio di Bartolomeo di Benedetto de' Landi, Biccherna panel, 1480. Siena, Archivio di Stato.

Figure 6. *The Miracle of the Doors.* Miniature, 1281–1284, from Alfonso X the Wise, *Cantigas de Santa María.* Florence, Biblioteca Nazionale Centrale, MS B. R. 20, fol. 2r.

The illuminator divided the leaf into six scenes, following a standard pattern: first we see the woman in front of the bolted door of the church, disappointed; then, as the darkness of the interior yawns before her, dimly lit by an oil lamp and a candelabra, astonished; and in the third panel gesturing with fresh astonishment before the same door, which has closed on its own and bolted itself shut. In this sequence the statue of the enthroned Virgin holding the Child that sits on the altar does not remain immobile, for the Madonna turns her head as she benevolently follows the movements of her worshipper and silently accepts her prayers, her offering, her regret.

Then we proceed to the woman's sense of bewilderment as she kneels before the closed gate of the city and prays for divine assistance with folded hands: and behold, the "Lady" miraculously appears on the threshold. Then we see the woman, now safe, in devout colloquy with the queen of heaven inside the city. Finally she preaches her story to all the people gathered in piety before the Virgin, who has shown herself so willing to listen. The church in the last scene is not, however, the one where the miracle took place, since it is located inside the city walls. And the sculpture on the altar is different, too, for the Madonna, rigidly frontal, now has one hand raised and is possibly holding a flower, while the Child is grasping a globe. In Santa María de los Mártires the Virgin's hand was lying loosely in her lap, and the attribute given to the Child was a book. The illuminator lets us follow arrivals and departures—the woman's entry into Santa María de los Mártires and her exit—by shifting the position of the tree near the facade of the church, and he knows how to use color effectively to measure her rising sense of fear and dismay and the reassuring effect of miraculous intervention. The door of the church is white, with only a partial strip of blackness suggesting the opening of one of its panels, and it turns white again when the woman leaves the building. The gate of the closed city is, in contrast, deeply and menacingly dark, but it acquires a golden tint when it becomes the backdrop to the Virgin who providentially appears. The Virgin raises up her protégée with the same gesture used in scenes of Christ in the Underworld at the moment when he sets Adam free, taking him by the wrist. This iconographic motif was well known to medieval spectators, and their recognition of it would have imparted particular intensity to the moment at which a miracle was encountered.

In the final scene the top part of the city tower appears, housing a large bell; the artist has crammed it into a corner directly above the half-open entrance to the church. Pealing imperiously, it is carrying into every street, into every house, the news that a great event has just taken place. In this scene we are, I repeat, in a church *inside* the city walls: only here can the miracle be properly announced and celebrated.

Not everyone in the Middle Ages was lucky enough to be lodged inside the city. New arrivals, merchants waiting for things to take a turn for the better, artisans, peasants, and street sellers might find no housing inside the rigid circle of stone,

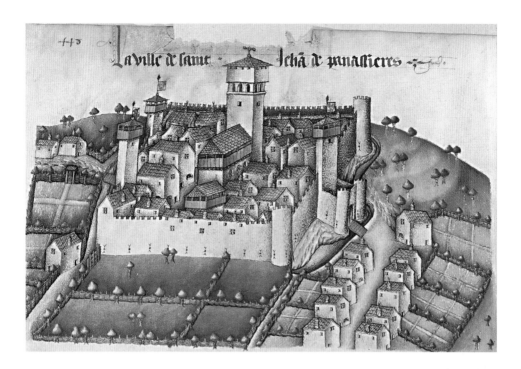

Figure 7. *View of Panissières in the Loire Valley with the* Borghi *near the City Walls.* Painting by Guillaume Revel, *Armorial,* fifteenth century. Paris, Bibliothèque Nationale, MS Fr. 22297, fol. 448.

Figure 8. *The* Borghi *near the City Walls.* Beato Angelico, detail from the *Pala di Santa Trinita,* tempera panel, 1437–c.1440. Florence, Museo di San Marco. Scala / Art Resource, NY.

where space was hoarded and strenuously defended. So like chicks gathered around a mother hen, their houses gathered outside the walls and formed *borghi,* usually rows of houses that were built on both sides of the radial roads leading away from the city (figs. 7–8). Then, when the city grew to the point of overflowing with people and wealth, a new ring of walls with an ampler diameter than the preceding one was thrown up around it, engrossing the recent settlements. At Siena, for example, the first circle of walls was demolished in 1256 and the *borghi* became part of the city.[11]

But neither your fellow human beings nor massive stonework could ever really keep you safe: for every human action in the Middle Ages, support from heaven was considered crucial. "If God does not guard my city, in vain the sentries watch" runs the second couplet of the beginning of Psalm 126, and a version of these words are still to be seen in the inscription placed on the civic tower at Volterra.[12] The heavenly court was called on to give visible protection: often the saints were depicted above the city gates named after them, for example at Florence, where Saint George rode on horseback above Porta San Giorgio (dating from 1324), in a sculpture that can still be seen.[13] The patron saints of the whole city were extremely potent as well; then there was Saint Peter, the keeper of the heavenly gates, with his corresponding attribute, a massive set of keys, and naturally, there was the Virgin Mary. The oldest statutes of Verona, dating from 1228, give orders that "on all the gates of the city of Verona, both those that are open at present and those that will be shortly, there should be depicted in memory of God and his blessed Genitrix Mary, one or more pictures of the glorious ever-virgin Mary with her merciful Son on her arm, the blessed Christopher and San Zeno our protectors, and Saint Peter with his keys in his hand" (fig. 9).[14] A disposition of the same tenor can be read in the statutes of Città di Castello from 1261: on all five gates of the city there shall be painted "as quickly as possible" the Virgin and Child, and Saint Christopher with the baby Jesus on his shoulders. It is recommended that the frescoes be of good quality so they will last, and stay beautiful, and that when they have been completed they should be well sheltered in such a way as to resist the destructive effects of rainwater.[15] The priors of the people at Foligno, for their part, had to ensure that every evening a lamp should be lit before the images of the Virgin and Saint Christopher at the foot of the staircase of their palazzo, and that there should always be enough oil (supplied at public expense) for the light to burn throughout the night.[16] At Osimo, in the Marche, the communal authorities made it their business to ensure that the gates of their city would bear painted images of the Virgin, "San" Benvenuto (who died in 1282 and who, despite his propitious name, which means "welcome," was never in fact canonized), and Saint Christopher. They went so far as to specify, in chapter 43 of their statute, the utility of the location: "at every single gate" (*in quaslibet portas*) where the traffic is heaviest, so that people should multiply their praises of Mary and these saints as they enter and leave (*ut ipsis a transeuntibus laudes inferantur*).[17]

Figure 9. *San Zeno, Patron of the City of Verona.* Sculpture, twelfth century. Verona, Church of San Zeno, lunette in the portal.

To gaze upon the image of Saint Christopher protected one from a bad death, in other words, against a sudden death, which was the obsession of the good Christian in the Middle Ages. An abrupt end might take a person straight to hell, for he would not have had the time to release himself from the burden of sin through repentance, confession, and penance.

The Passion of Saint Christopher is a succession of improbable happenings and horrendous tortures, each of them victoriously endured.[18] Under interrogation, Christopher had declared that his name, Reprobus (reprobate), had been changed following his baptism to Christophorus, meaning "he who carries Christ." Out of this play on words, which reads the name in real, not spiritual terms (as the literal meaning of the Greek, "to carry Christ," allows)[19] was constructed the legend of his conversion. He was a Canaanite of gigantic size and terrible appearance. Having decided to serve only the most powerful prince in the world he passed successively from the service of the king of the country to that of the Devil, until the latter revealed to him that there existed another and much more powerful lord, namely, Christ. So the giant set out to look for him. In order to ingratiate himself and hasten the moment of the encounter, Christopher, counseled by a hermit, began to help voyagers cross a great river that flowed not far from the hermit's hut. Using a tree trunk as a staff, Christopher traversed the river in both directions repeatedly.

Then one day he took a baby on his shoulders, but during the crossing the current swelled dangerously, while the baby grew heavier and heavier. After much struggle the pair reached the far bank, and Christopher discovered, to his joy, the reason for so much difficulty: he had been carrying on his shoulders the baby Jesus.

Simply to look at Saint Christopher was a guarantee of safety: it was enough to fix your gaze on his image as soon as you awoke and you could be sure that during the whole of that day you would be protected from sudden death.[20] So his image had to be visible at a distance: for that reason the frescoes that portray Christopher are normally of large size, and visibility is also promoted by the huge stature of the helpful Canaanite. In the Palazzo Pubblico of Siena, on the external wall of the Capella Nova in the embrasure of the Anticoncistoro, the imposing figure of Christopher looms up, five meters tall, painted by Taddeo di Bartolo, with his legs, which would otherwise block the doorway beneath, disappearing into the waves (fig. 10).[21] A list of all the Saint Christophers painted at Siena in the Palazzo del Comune, dry perhaps but statistically telling, will confirm how urgently the need for holy protection was felt. The first attestation is dated 1296; the painter is Bindo di Diotisalvi;[22] eight years later a maestro Mino is again at work on the same subject;[23] in 1320 Lippo Memmi is mentioned,[24] and in 1323 Simone Martini.[25] The Saint Christopher of Taddeo di Bartolo, the only one of the frescoes on the list that survives, forms part of the prominent cycle with which the painter covered all the walls of the Anticoncistoro from 1408 to 1414. The saintly giant is also, however, the only one to be cited by name in the epigraph that adorns the work, on account of the apotropaic value of his image: "Taddeo di Bartolo of Siena painted this chapel in 1407 with the figure of Saint Christopher and these other figures."[26] And in other civic buildings or on the walls of churches, frequently on a facade or on the gates of a city, Saint Christopher is available for the benefit of the public—but not only there. Opportunely scaled down, he also meets us in a fifteenth-century fresco (one of many that could easily be cited) as we climb the steep stairs of Palazzo Davanzati (originally Davizzi) in Florence,[27] and he even turns up transformed into an amulet, sewed onto items of clothing or painted upon objects of every sort.[28] Given his specialization, Saint Christopher became the patron saint of those who operated ferries, and by extension he was also the patron of voyagers, pilgrims, and merchants. "S[anctus] Chri[st]oforus merchatorum" (Saint Christopher of the merchants) is his appellation in the inscription on a panel painting of 1377 signed and dated by Giovanni di Bologna, and commissioned by the Scuola dei Mercanti of Venice.[29] In popular prints of the fifteenth century, the image of the saint is normally accompanied by an inscription in Latin, a maxim of sorts, often with assonances or capricious rhymes; here are some examples: "Look upon Christopher and then you will be safe"; "Saint Christopher, your virtues are many; he who beholds you in the

Figure 10. *Saint Christopher*. Taddeo di Bartolo, fresco, c. 1414. Siena, Palazzo Pubblico, Anticoncistoro. Scala / Art Resource, NY.

Figure 11. *Saint Christopher, with an Animalesque Face*. Miniature, from a *Martyrologium,* twelfth century. Stuttgart, Landesbibliothek, MS Hist. Fol. 415, fol. 50r.

morning will be laughing at night"; "Whoever the image of Saint Christopher sees, will certainly not die a bad death that same day."[30] An inscription of this type, more modest in that it expresses contentment simply at being protected by Christopher against illness for one day, is placed at the feet of the ferryman in a panel painting of Niccolò di Tommaso from the second half of the fourteenth century, located today in the Walters Art Gallery of Baltimore.[31] Even when squeezed into the dimensions of a miniature (fig. 11), Christopher retains his gigantic size: he is taller than the loftiest towers of a city (fragile things that he clasps), and his feet fill the entire space of the wide-open gates in the walls. The illuminator, recalling the terrible visage that the legend attributes to the saint, has given him the muzzle of a ferocious lion, but the citizens who appear in throngs at the windows and on the parapets show no sign of fear and greet him with trusting gestures. The inscription reads: "Sanctus Christophorus Chananeus."

Like Christopher, Julian was another powerful saint who protected wayfarers (in Italian, Giuliano; fig. 12); that his existence is entirely legendary makes no difference. In a burst of rage at finding, as he thought, his wife and her lover in the conjugal bed,

Julian had killed the sleeping couple, only to find that they were actually his own parents, who had arrived for an unexpected visit, and to whom his wife had given the marital chamber. As penance Julian and his wife (who, as a wife, was automatically implicated) built a hospice and hospital to take in wayfarers, for whom they cared with a great deal of charity and self-sacrifice. One evening, during a storm, Julian saved a leper at risk of drowning, cared for him, and put him to sleep in his own bed. The leper, who was actually Christ, was cured, and suddenly vanished, but not before announcing to the couple that they would soon be rewarded for their devotion.

Julian is the main subject of the conversation between a group of fake merchants, actually "thieves of a disreputable sort," and the incautious Rinaldo d'Asti, who joins up with them along the road as he is returning home, in a novella from the *Decameron*. Boccaccio narrates this with great gusto for the special benefit of "those who journey along the uncertain roads of love, where those who do not regularly say the Our Father of St. Julian may very often find a good bed but a bad lodging."[32]

As they traveled along, with the conversation, as it usually does, passing from one thing to another, they came to the topic of prayers that men offer to God. One of the bandits, of which there were three, asked Rinaldo, 'What about you, sir? What kind of prayer do you normally say when you are traveling?' To this question Rinaldo replied,

Figure 12. *Saint Julian.* Wing of a polyptych by an assistant of Bernardo Daddi, fourteenth century. Barga (Lucca), Conservatorio di Santa Elisabetta.

"To tell the truth, I am a rather simple and down-to-earth sort in these matters; I'm the old-fashioned kind of guy who calls them as he sees them, and I know very few prayers; nevertheless, it is my usual practice when traveling never to leave an inn in the morning without saying one to Our Father and one Hail Mary for the souls of St. Julian's mother and father, after which I pray to God and to St. Julian to grant me a suitable lodging for the coming night. And in my journeys I have often found myself in grave danger, from which I have nonetheless managed to escape and find myself in a safe place with good lodgings that same evening; so I firmly believe that St. Julian, in whose honor I say my prayers, has obtained this favor for me through his intercession with God, and if I had not recited my prayer that morning, I don't think I could manage to travel safely during the day or arrive safely by nightfall."

"Did you say your prayers this morning?" wondered the man who had asked the question. "Yes, of course," replied Rinaldo.[33]

Here we can leave Rinaldo to his adventures (fig. 13), which will have a happy ending (see p. 166 below), because a woman, a beautiful widow, will intervene to compensate the poor follower of Saint Julian after he has been robbed by his evil traveling companions and left trembling with cold, shoeless, and dressed only in a shirt.

Figure 13. *Rinaldo d'Asti Is Attacked in the Woods by Fake Merchants.* Miniature, late fourteenth century, from Boccaccio, *Decameron* 2.2. Vienna, Österreichische Nationalbibliothek, MS 2561, fol. 49r.

Anyone on a voyage, all those who had to travel on business or those on a pilgrimage, felt that they were in a permanently precarious state, exposed to the attacks of wolves, stray dogs, sometimes even bears, but above all, brigands. Or they might abruptly encounter a sortie by armed men who were on the move because of the countless wars and small-scale conflicts.[34] Even in the extraordinary cavalcade that winds through Gentile da Fabriano's altarpiece of the Adoration of the Magi (fig. 14) with an interminable, lavish procession of knights, servants, and animals of every sort, even apes and trained leopards, violence and death find a place. The parade of exotic costumes and golden harness, the whirl of color and jeweled clasps, of plumed and outlandish headgear, dwindles away into a background of familiar

Figure 14. *Adoration of the Magi.* Gentile da Fabriano, tempera panel, 1423. Florence, Uffizi. Scala/Art Resource, NY.

Figure 15. *An Assassination.* Detail from fig. 14, Gentile da Fabriano, *Adoration of the Magi,* tempera panel, 1423. Florence, Uffizi. Scala / Art Resource, NY.

Western European cities with walls, battlements, and towers. Yet the marvelous excursion also includes a small episode of quotidian reality: two soldiers have taken an unlucky victim, alone and on foot, by surprise outside the city walls and are finishing him off with their daggers (fig. 15).

Wars, death, destruction occurring in the city, in the countryside, in the small villages—these are the images that fill the whole fresco of *Il Mal Governo: Gli effetti in città* (Bad Government. The Effects in the City) by Ambrogio Lorenzetti at Siena, and they reflect a widespread feeling of dread encapsulated in the sword of Timor (Fear; fig. 16), a skeletal, leering old woman soaring across the broad expanse of *Tirannide*

(Tyranny) in a dark and menacing sky lit up by the flames of the burning villages. Peace, justice, and concord do reign, but only in the ideology of the Nine, the magistracy that then governed Siena,[35] who commissioned the fresco from Lorenzetti as their political manifesto. The diminutive aerial figure of Securitas (Security; fig. 17)

Figure 16. Timor (*Fear*). Ambrogio Lorenzetti, detail from *Bad Government. The Effects in the City* (*Il Buon Governo. Gli effetti in città*), fresco, 1338–1339. Siena, Palazzo Pubblico, Sala della Pace. Scala/Art Resource, NY.

Figure 17. Securitas (*Security*). Ambrogio Lorenzetti, detail from *Good Government. The Effects in the Countryside* (*Il Buon Governo. Gli effetti in campagna*), fresco, 1338–1339. Siena, Palazzo Pubblico, Sala della Pace. Scala/Art Resource, NY

Figure 18. *A Young Boy Steals a Candle, Urged On by an Impish Devil.* Benedetto Bonfigli, detail from the *Gonfalone di san Bernardino da Siena,* tempera panel, 1465. Perugia, Galleria Nazionale dell'Umbria.

above the delightful countryside of the *Buon Governo* declares forthrightly on her scroll: "Let every free man travel without fear / and let each one work and sow / who over the commune / will preserve this lady [Justice] in lordship: for she has deprived the wicked of all power." But at the same time Securitas is displaying a gallows from which a hanged man swings, as an eloquent reminder that the Nine know how to act ruthlessly when necessary. Scoundrels and bandits will be dealt exemplary punishment. A similar warning is also contained in the "Gonfalone di San Bernardino" of 1465, where the painter Benedetto Bonfigli depicts a lad stealing candles, while a devil eggs him on (fig. 18), but at the same time, to reassure the viewer, condemns him with the words "Fura che serai apeso" (Steal and you will be hung!).[36]

Figure 19. *An Itinerant Peddler.* Ambrogio Lorenzetti, detail from *Good Government. The Effects in the Countryside (Il Buon Governo. Gli effetti in campagna)*, fresco, 1338–1339. Siena, Palazzo Pubblico, Sala della Pace. Scala/Art Resource, NY.

There is at least one man, though, lost in a tawny field of ripe wheat, who does not trust the proclamation of Securitas. He is by trade an itinerant peddler (fig. 19), and he has a sack over one shoulder and a portable display case slung diagonally across his torso, on which he has laid out, more to impress the viewer than some unlikely client, his wares: collars, belts, colored ribbons. Attached to his belt and clearly visible there is a pointed dagger, for his presumably small profits are no guarantee against the danger of aggression. This individual barely catches the eye, and for just that reason might be an autonomous interjection by Lorenzetti, a deviation from the commission he was given by the Nine, who wanted him to concentrate all the killing, depredation, and devastation exclusively on the wall dedicated to *Il Mal Governo,* with its ruined cities and bare uncultivated fields, where the words of Timor are punctually made real: "None passes this way except in fear of death, for there is robbery within and without the gates."

Both Securitas and Timor refer insistently to the roads because the effective functioning of the communications network, bringing prosperity and life, was felt to be indispensable for the city's existence, and for this reason the roads—in paintings and on the statute books at any rate—were kept in perfect condition, free of all hazard. The circulation of goods provided the commune with a double benefit, through the payment of tolls and through the availability of the goods themselves. The roads were indispensable for providing the city with foodstuffs and keeping the local market supplied. The sources insist particularly on this last point: the population, massed within the restricted ambit of the walls, felt that the practicability of the roadways was essential for its own survival. Since modern methods of preserving food were unknown, victuals in large quantities had necessarily to be brought in from the countryside every day, in every season and all weathers, no matter how cold or wet. It didn't take much to turn the potholes into sloughs and the packed earth into an impassable bed of mud!

In 1290, it was decided to brick over all the streets of Siena because the side streets, which were unbricked, were spilling filth and mud[37] into the thoroughfares, which were already "paved" (with bricks, that is, not stones).[38] In the portion of Lorenzetti's fresco *Il Buon Governo. Gli Effetti del Buon Governo in campagna* (Good Government. The Effects in the Countryside), we see wide and well-kept roads (fig. 20) dividing fields and hills into a sinuous checkerboard, exactly the way the magistracy for the roads of Siena and the surrounding district prescribed that they should.[39] In the foreground an imposing caravan of men and mules loaded with bales of wool and cloth is traversing a handsome bridge made of brick (fig. 21) with three arches (not some rudimental and rickety wooden structure), while other bridges of the same type can be made out in the distance. The road leading into the city (fig. 22) is paved with stone as it approaches the walls and reinforced by a low unmortared

Figure 20. *Good Government. The Effects in the Countryside (Il Buon Governo. Gli effetti in campagna)*, Ambrogio Lorenzetti, fresco, 1338–1339. Siena, Palazzo Pubblico, Sala della Pace. Scala/Art Resource, NY.

Figure 21. *A Train of Men with Mules Crosses a Bridge Made of Brick*. Ambrogio Lorenzetti, detail from *Good Government. The Effects in the Countryside (Buon Governo. Gli effetti in campagna)*, fresco, 1338–1339. Siena, Palazzo Pubblico, Sala della Pace. Scala/Art Resource, NY.

Figure 22. *A Road Paved with Flagstones near the Walls of the City*. Ambrogio Lorenzetti, detail from *Good Government. The Effects in the Countryside (Buon Governo. Gli effetti in campagna)*, fresco, 1338–1339. Siena, Palazzo Pubblico, Sala della Pace. Scala/Art Resource, NY.

wall. Along the road people and animals flow in both directions, nobles setting out into the countryside on horseback to hunt with falcons and peasants bringing their wares into the city (among them a fine-looking pig with a characteristic band of white on its coat, a typically Sienese variety known today as *cinta,* "banded"). They

Figure 23. *The Martyrdom of San Marco during a Fierce Hailstorm.* Beato Angelico, detail from the *Tabernacolo dei Linaioli,* tempera panel, 1433. Florence, Museo di San Marco. Scala/Art Resource, NY.

Figure 24. *Lightning Bolts Raining Down.* Miniature, 1281–1284 (detail), from Alfonso X the Wise, *Cantigas de Santa María.* Florence, Biblioteca Nazionale Centrale, MS B. R. 20, fol. 101r. Scala/Art Resource, NY.

make their way alone or in small groups conversing quietly, behind mules and donkeys with sacks of flour or grain on their packsaddles, while a blind beggar, hunched at the edge of the road, shows his empty eye sockets and hopes. All of the vast landscape is illuminated by the sun; contentment and sunshine fill the city of Siena, the city of the *Buon Governo,* that is, just as the broad sweep of country beams with the fertility that comes from hard work in the fields.

Agricultural work went on all year, and one hailstorm could put it at risk, even destroy a crop altogether. The pellets of ice raining down amid thunder and lightning (fig. 23) were considered to be the work of demons, the weapon they used to vent their rancor as defeated rebel angels. (The Virgin Mary brought a halt once, in the indeterminate time of miracle, to an eruption of Mount Etna, an eruption that an illuminator represented as a rain of lightning bolts; fig. 24).[40]

The abode of the devils is in the sky, at around three miles above the earth, in a stratum of air lying between the clear and tepid one close to the earth and the very hot one close to the sun, explained the Dominican Giordano da Pisa in a sermon inspired by the lines of Genesis, "In the beginning God created the heavens and the earth":

> The air in the middle, they say it is very cold, and is dark, and is so cold that if someone found themselves there, in no way could they survive. . . . And this is that place, according to what the learned say, where the hail and the snow are generated, and the rainfalls. . . . The saints tell that the Inferno of the demonry, and their place, is there in this cold tenebrous air. Whence, say the saints, in this air a large number of them abide; inasmuch as it suits them, for they are not worthy to stay in air of light, but rather of shadows, for they themselves are tenebrous; and because of the coldness too, for all of them are cold in love of God.[41]

Pious amulets had the power to counteract the ever-present menace of storms and hail. The chronicler Opicino de Canistris recounts in his work in praise of Pavia in 1330 that on the feast day of Saint Agatha, 5 February, during the mass, specifically, during the reading of the Gospel, "The little boys write *brevia*[42] in which are comprised those words that the angel of God wrote on the marble tablet of the sepulcher of this virgin: 'Mentem sanctam, spontaneam, honorem Deo et patrie liberationem' [Saintly spontaneous mind, honor of God and liberation of our city]. They place these *brevia* in the fields and in the vineyards so that they may be freed from the danger of tempests and hail."[43] A year after the death of Agatha, a powerful volcanic eruption that "descended on the city [of Catania] like an impetuous torrent and loosened stones and earth"[44] was miraculously brought to a halt by the veil that covered the sepulcher of the martyr. For this reason Saint Agatha was a valid protector against the uncontrollable forces of nature. In an unattributed fresco from the

end of the fourteenth or the beginning of the fifteenth century in the Palazzo Comunale of Lucignano (fig. 25),[45] Agatha holds in one hand a cup containing her excised breasts, the characterizing attribute of her martyrdom, and in the other a scroll on which are displayed the words of the angel.

The words traced by the angel in marble were often repeated in the bronze of bells. To give a few examples: in 1239 the *breve* was carved on the bell of the bell tower of the Basilica Superiore of Assisi,[46] and in 1438 on a bell at Foligno.[47] The holy peals (fig. 26) coming from the house of God would have been enough on their own to put the invisible army of demons to flight: reinforced by the words inscribed on the bronze, their talismanic power was irresistible. As William Durant[48] reassuringly explained, "The bells sound their blessing to drive the hostile armies of the Enemy and all his ambushes far away, to distance the crash of the hail, the whirling storm wind, the onrush of the tempest and

Figure 25. *Saint Agatha and the Breve.* Anonymous, fresco, fifteenth century (?), Lucignano (Arezzo), Palazzo Comunale, Sala dell'Udienza.

Figure 26. *A Wedding, with Twin Bells Pealing in a Bell Tower.* Color drawing, fifteenth century, from *Esopo in volgare.* Florence, Biblioteca Nazionale Centrale, MS II, II, 85, fol. 9r.

the lightning, the threatening roar, so that the whirlwinds should cease and the spirits of the storm and the Powers of the air should be fought back and conquered." As a tyrant grows frightened when he hears the trumpet of the army of a powerful enemy king, concludes William Durant, so do the devils flee, filled with fear, when they hear the trumpet blast of the church militant, the bells.[49]

Chapter Three

INSIDE THE CITY

BUYING AND SELLING

Cities today still have their noise and their smells, which are both generated for the most part by automobile traffic and general pollution. The voices of human beings, on the other hand, have fallen almost completely silent in public; no one sings any more unless they are a bit eccentric, and even the artisans, who until not so long ago used to whistle or sing while they worked, are quiet now, preferring to listen to the recorded voices and music of others. At most they utter outbursts of impatience. Certainly no poet could any longer expect, as Dante Alighieri could, to hear his verses being sung. One day in Florence Dante had left the house after eating, and while passing through Porta San Pietro, came upon "a smith who was beating iron on the anvil and singing Dante the way one sings a popular poem, and mixing his verses up, shortening some and lengthening others, so that it seemed to Dante that he was receiving a great injury from the fellow." Without a word Dante went into the man's workshop and threw his tongs, his hammer, his balances, and all his other implements into the street. When the smith remonstrated loudly at finding himself stripped of the tools of his trade and blocked from exercising his own special skill, the poet replied, "'You are singing from my work, but not the way I wrote it; I have no other art, and you are ruining it for me.' The irate smith, at a loss for words, gathered up his things and went back to his work; and after that, when he wanted to sing, he sang of Tristan and Lancelot, and left Dante alone."[1] The heroes Tristan and

Lancelot had a role in medieval art as well: the museum of Palazzo Davanzati at Florence includes a coverlet (fig. 27) of Sicilian manufacture from the end of the fourteenth century embroidered with eight stories about Tristan,[2] while a miniature showing Lancelot engaged in a duel is preserved in a codex from the end of the thirteenth century, copied in Italy (fig. 28).[3]

On another occasion we meet the poet in Florence wearing a full suit of armor—which we might think unusual, but which was actually not out of place in the dangerous streets of the city: "And wearing armor to protect his throat and his arm,[4] as people then customarily did," the poet saw a donkey driver transporting garbage, "who was going along behind the donkeys singing the book of Dante, and when he had sung for a bit, he hit the donkey and said 'Arri (Giddyup).'" Dante

Figure 27. *Tales of Tristan.* Embroidered coverlet, fourteenth century. Florence, Museo di Palazzo Davanzati.

Figure 28. *Lancelot Engaged in a Duel.* Miniature, late thirteenth century, from Rustichello da Pisa, *Romanzo arturiano.* Paris, Bibliothèque Nationale, MS 1463, fol. 60v.

accosted him and dealt him a forceful blow on the shoulder with his mailed fist, say-ing, 'I didn't put that *Arrì* in there.'" A lively dispute ensued, with bad language and obscene gestures on the part of the donkey driver, and insulting remarks on the part of Dante.[5] The poor smith, rebuked and reduced to singing only about "Tristan and

Figure 29. *The Wife of Duke Guernieri Plays Chess with the Knight Guglielmo and Attempts to Seduce Him.* Detail from the frescos of the cycle of *La Châtelaine de Vergy,* late fourteenth century. Florence, Museo di Palazzo Davanzati. Scala / Art Resource, NY.

Lancelot," testifies to the popularity of adventure romances, not only in precious manuscripts, which were often illuminated, but also in well-known poems or in simple songs, and accounts for the fact that these heroes turn up in frescoes painted in rich bourgeois houses. In Florence the story of Tristan and Isolde had been painted in the fourteenth-century house of the Teri;[6] the "story of the woman of Virzir and of messer Guglielmo," translated into Florentine rhyming verse in the fourteenth century from the French romance of *La Châtelaine de Vergy*[7] was painted—and is still preserved—in the bedchamber of the present Palazzo Davanzati for the wedding in 1395 of Francesco Tommaso Davizzi with Catalana degli Alberti (fig. 29).

Another human voice that has disappeared from the modern city is that of the itinerant sellers of small luxury items and decorations, hawking their wares to women and to men in need of presents to give to their sweethearts: "The pedlar goes off with her basket, jingling her bells, dangling her jewellry, rings, and pins, saying 'Tablecloths for sale, swap them for towels.'"[8] Juan Ruiz, archpriest of Hita, who describes this woman, must have known her well and been a habitual customer: to a shepherd girl he promises "a pendant and a brooch and a rabbit-skin bag"; to a

"mountain girl," as gifts in the (unlikely) event that she marries, "a hair clasp of vermilion ribbon . . . a fine tambourine, six rings of tin . . . earrings and a brass clasp . . .
and a yellow bonnet with stripes at the front, and some knee-high boots" To win
over highborn ladies, more impressive presents were necessary, not merely "fine
cloth or girdles, nor beads, nor rings, nor gloves."[9]

DISCUSSIONS AND ARGUMENTS

People in the Middle Ages spent a lot of time together, in the streets with their
neighbors. We get a description of that life from an elderly Parisian husband who, to
guide his young wife, offered her an ancient Roman lady, Lucretia, as an edifying
example of conjugal virtue. To make his account more vivid and incisive he tells her
the story of the unexpected return to Rome of Lucretia's husband Collatinus and
his comrades, who had been detained until then by a siege. The setting within which
these ancient Romans move is perfectly medieval: they find some of their wives
intent on gossip and others engaged in playing cards or other amusements or busy
killing time with their neighbors. "Those who had dined together were singing
or telling fables and stories, or else were amusing themselves with guessing games.
Yet others were in the street with their neighbors playing *tiers* and *bric* and other
games of the same kind—except for Lucretia, who was inside. She had wool workers
in a large room far from the street, in the most withdrawn part of the house, and
there she sat alone and apart, at a distance from her workers, devoutly holding a
book. With her countenance lowered she was reciting the Hours, piously and very
humbly."[10]

Dealers and artisans for the most part had their shops in the houses they lived in,
on the ground floor, and displayed their products in the street on counters made of
wood, or built into the wall of the house. The shop itself, in order to exploit to the
maximum the space available, was often equipped with shelving for storing the merchandise, hanging up the tools, or perhaps even for use by the apprentices as a kind
of bunk bed.

A lively novella by Sacchetti shows us very clearly the contiguity between house
and workshop, and also the assembly-line methods of the painters, whose works,
when seen today by visitors in the rooms of a museum or by devout persons in the
religious quiet of a church, may seem unique and particularly inspired. A Sienese
painter, Mino, was being cuckolded by his wife. One night he was forced to remain
outside the city on account of a job, and the wife took advantage of this to bring her
lover into the house. A relative of the painter, who knew about the affair, immediately decided to go and alert the betrayed husband, but it was not easy to get out of
the city, since night had fallen; he had to assure the guards that he would be returning soon and convinced them to leave the *sportello,* the smallest entrance, open. So

Mino reentered, and when he got home he began searching the whole place, but his wife had found a special way to conceal her paramour:

> This Mino was a painter of crucifixes more than anything else, and especially of the
> kind that were carved to bring the figures into relief. There were always some in the
> house, either finished or in progress, sometimes four, sometimes six [fig. 30], and he
> kept them, as painters usually do, on a table or long workbench in his shop, leaning
> against the wall one beside the other, each covered with a large towel. At the moment
> he had six, four of them carved and sculpted, and two painted on the flat surface; and
> all of them were on a workbench that was two braccia in height, leaning against the
> wall one beside the other, and each of them covered with a large towel or other linen
> cloth.[11]

The wife's lover becomes the seventh, living, crucifix, covered with linen. His hope of passing undetected depends on the fact that fourteenth-century artists

Figure 30. *An Artist in His Workshop*. Miniature, c. 1470, from G. Boccaccio, *Des clères et nobles femmes*. New York, New York Public Library, Spencer Collection, MS 33, fol. 37v.

customarily practiced painting, sculpture, and woodworking all at the same time: mixing the colors, sawing and carving the wood—what a lot of dust these activities must have created in the workshop, if it was necessary to be so careful to cover up the works in progress! Mino's quarry eluded him that night, but the lover remained a prisoner in the room. "This workshop had a front door that was locked with a key from outside, because a young assistant to Mino opened it every morning, just like the other shops; and there was a small door to the domestic quarters at the other end, which Mino used when he entered the shop. When he left the shop to return to the domestic quarters, he closed this small door with a key."[12] The lover couldn't get out into the street because the door giving onto the street had been closed from the outside by the assistant, and he couldn't go back through the house because Mino, when leaving the workshop through the little internal door that led to the domestic quarters, had closed it behind him with his key.[13]

The shortage of space in the interiors drove people out of doors; the streets became ever more narrow, even as they became more animated, because men and women stopped in front of the counters to buy, to make contracts, to chat, perhaps, with a member of the household who had come to the window of one of the upper stories. You could say that both people and things were driven outdoors by the need for more space and light. Women liked to be at the window or on the balcony (fig. 31), or seated in the loggia to work or to arrange their hair.[14] The washing was hung on external poles on the facade to dry; awnings to shelter the rooms from the glare of the sun fluttered from the same poles (in order to save space they did not use blinds inside, as we do in our houses). During the day a cage with a pet bird inside might be hung from a nail in the window opening, and countless other objects and heavy loads were hung from poles, hooks, and chains on the external walls (fig. 32). Vases large and small, with sweet-smelling herbs and flowers, were placed on the cornices and corbels of the windows, on terraces, and even on tiled roof drains; some of them were balanced very precariously indeed, while others were set on ingenious corbels with folding legs, like suspended gardens (fig. 33). Lorenzetti's fresco of the *Buon Governo* shows many of the details just mentioned, even a cat moving along an external pole to get from one room to another; it also includes a couple of counters, one belonging to a man offering salami and cold drinks, the other to a man selling footwear (fig. 34).[15] The former has hung sausages and dried meats, all of them well salted (the kind of snack that makes you thirsty), on a pole attached to two corbels protruding from the wall, while on the counter top he has placed pitchers, glasses, bottles, and a cask. The latter has hung stockings fitted with soles[16] from the usual pole, while a selection of shoes, some on lasts and others that are being worked on, together with the tools of his trade, are scattered on the counter. For that matter, medieval shops of this kind have been preserved to this day in the town of Spoleto (fig. 35).[17]

Figure 31. *Women on a Balcony, with Vases of Odoriferous Herbs.* Agnolo Gaddi, fresco, second half of the fifteenth century, from *La leggenda del Sacro Cingolo.* Prato, Duomo, Cappella del Sacro Cingolo. Scala/Art Resource, NY.

Figure 32. *Multistory Houses with Poles at the Windows.* Masolino and Masaccio, detail from *La resurrezione di Tabita e il miracolo dello storpio.* Fresco, late fifteenth century. Florence, Santa Maria del Carmine, Cappella Brancacci. Scala/Art Resource, NY.

Figure 33. *Birth of the Virgin, with a Medieval Roof Garden in the Background.* Maestro della Madonna Cini, panel, fourteenth century. Lausanne, Musée Cantonal des Beaux Arts.

Figure 34. *Artisans and Shopkeepers Displaying Their Wares on Wooden Counters.* Ambrogio Lorenzetti, detail from *Good Government. The Effects in the City* (*Il Buon Governo. Gli effetti in città*), fresco, 1338–1339. Siena, Palazzo Pubblico, Sala della Pace. Scala/Art Resource, NY.

Figure 35. *Medieval Shops in the "Stradetta" in Spoletto.* Via del Palazzo dei Duchi, Spoleto.

One could go into the street to buy fish, which were kept live in special containers (fig. 36), meat (fig. 37), green vegetables, bread; but there were pieces of furniture, kitchen utensils, fabrics on offer, too—a little bit of everything, in fact. In a
well-known miniature (fig. 38) from the early fifteenth century showing the market
at Porta Ravegnana in Bologna, there is a rich selection of merchandise on display.
Reading from top to bottom, we see scattered on the ground and on the counters
pots and pans, fabrics, chests, pails and tubs, a much sought-after "seggetta" (a toilet
stool), a grate, andirons and a cauldron for the fireplace, more fabrics, readymade
suits, headgear of many sorts, piles of dressed skins, and casks.

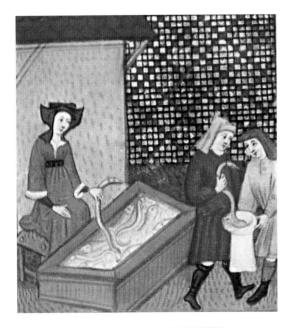

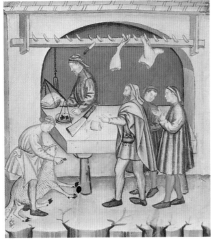

Figure 36. *Selling Fish in the Street.* Miniature,
late fourteenth century, from Boccaccio,
Decameron 9.8. Vienna, Österreichische
Nationalbibliothek, MS 2561, fol. 340v.

Figure 37. *A Butcher's Shop, Specializing in
Mutton.* Miniature, late fourteenth century,
from the *Tacuinum Sanitatis.* Rome, Biblioteca Casanatense, MS 4182, fol. 138.

Given how difficult it was to keep food for long, people had to buy it in small quantities daily, so every day the flow of shoppers brought the city to life. If you felt tired you could take a seat on the stone benches placed against the houses for that purpose (fig. 39). An evocation of civility in urban life enlivens a novella by Boccaccio, with a protagonist named Cisti, whom "though endowed with the noblest of spirits, Fortune made into a baker" (fig. 40). Every day Cisti watched important people walk past his shop, among them Messer Geri and the ambassadors of the pope, and "since it was very hot outside, it occurred to him that it would be a fine act of courtesy on his part to offer them some of his good white wine." Cisti dared not make an explicit offer, given the difference in social class, but he found a way to induce the passing nobles themselves to ask for something to quench their thirst. So "every morning, always wearing a shiny white doublet and a freshly washed apron, which made Cisti look more like a miller than a baker, around the hour he thought Messer Geri would be passing by with the emissaries, at the entrance of his shop he

Figure 38. *The Market at Porta Ravegnana in Bologna.* Miniature, beginning of the fifteenth century, from the *Matricolae Societatis Draperorum,* no. 93. Bologna, Museo Civico. Scala/Art Resource, NY.

Figure 39. *A Lover Climbing a Ladder.* Stone benches are positioned at either side of the front door. Miniature, fifteenth century, from Boccaccio, *Decameron* 3.3. Paris, Bibliothèque de l'Arsenal, MS 5070, fol. 103v.

Figure 40. *The Courtesy of Cisti the Baker.* Miniature, fifteenth century, from Boccaccio, *Decameron* 6.2. Paris, Bibliothèque de l'Arsenal, MS 5070, fol. 223v.

would have set up a shiny tin pail of fresh water and a new but small Bolognese flask of his good white wine along with two glasses that gleamed so brightly they looked like silver." Taking a seat he began to drink. When at last Messer Geri was drawn to ask if he and his friends might taste that wine, which seemed so good, Cisti, "immediately had a fine-looking bench brought from inside the bakery and begged them to be seated," and then he himself "washed four beautiful new glasses and had a small decanter of his good wine brought forth, and then with meticulous care he poured the wine for Messer Geri and his companions."[18]

Men liked to be in the streets and the piazzas, doing business, making purchases, talking and arguing about things. And it might happen that a mouse might come to cause turmoil, as happened one July morning in Florence to Matteo di Cantino Cavalcanti. This man, who was old and very fat, was wearing "short stockings" that came up to his knees because of the hot weather and large breeches, "the old-fashioned kind, flared out at the bottom" (*coi gambuli larghi in giuso*). "There were gentlemen and merchants exchanging news in a circle in the piazza of the Mercato Nuovo, and this Matteo was a part of the circle. A group of young people chanced to come along, employees of the bankers who operate there, with a trap in which they had a mouse they had captured; and with their brooms in their hands, they halted in the middle of the piazza." These youngsters, no longer free to play around because they now worked for the money dealers but wanting to have a bit of fun chasing the mouse, opened the cage, and the terrorized animal fled up Matteo's breeches, causing a commotion. Sacchetti moralizes: it takes nothing to scare a man, even a man of great pomp and haughtiness. "He will bolt from fleas, and an assault by a mouse will put him beside himself."[19] Fleas and mice are intruders who ruin the image of self-possessed "gentlemen and merchants" sitting and discussing affairs!

Nostalgia was a bond that united men, who so often had had to leave their home city for business reasons or because they had been banished: "I, the writer, found myself in the city of Genoa a number of years ago, taking part in a large circle composed of many sagacious men from many places, in the piazza of the merchants. Among them was Messer Giovanni dell'Agnello and some of his associates, and several Florentines banished from Florence, and Lucchesi who could no longer remain in Lucca, and a few Sienese who could no longer remain in Siena; there were even some Genovesi present. There they began to talk about the sort of empty things that provide fodder for those far from home: stories, fibs, expressions of longing, and even astrological prognostications."[20]

BELLS AND "UPROAR"

Today the games that children used to play outside have disappeared, just as children themselves, with their shrieks and their loud complaints, have virtually gone from the streets. Even the bells (fig. 41) have fallen silent, ringing out only occasionally on Sunday, as though from a distance.

But in the Middle Ages the bells were essential for city life, beating out the rhythm of day and night with their peals, announcing political assemblies and festivals. One of these was marked by "a great triumph of bells and horns," as Marchionne di Coppo Stefani noted with satisfaction in his *Cronaca fiorentina*.[21] They also signaled, however, the urgent danger of a fire or an uprising: during the turbulent period of the Revolt of the Ciompi, a Sienese brigade on horseback got as far as Figline, in Florentine territory, but finding the gate of the city closed, "turned around, and, keeping close together and with great fear, went through the forest and got back to Gaiuole [in Sienese territory]. But if a bell had just rung out behind them, not one of them would have got away," is Marchionne's sarcastic comment.[22] In Florence in 1307 the commune threatened the monks of the Badia with the destruction of their bell tower right down to its foundations ("and did destroy almost half of it") "because they had sounded it" and made the "underclass" (literally the *popolo minuto* or "little people") and the "ruffians" run to their aid, provoking a "furious" skirmish.[23] During the "War of the Eight Saints" in 1377, Macerata had been attacked several times by the troops of Captain Lutz von Landau, a German mercenary. One night a huge storm blocked the drains and flooded the houses, and a woman, suddenly finding the water rising around her, started to cry for help. Her pleas unleashed a general panic, because the sound of the bells ringing brought everyone out of their houses, convinced that the enemy was at the gates. One of the novellas of Sacchetti relates this story, with what degree of historical accuracy we need not enquire—everyone knew what it was like when the alarm sounded:

Figure 41. *A Bellman at Work*. Miniature, middle of the thirteenth century, from Matthew Paris, *Vita Sancti Albani*. Dublin, Trinity College, MS 177, fol. 63.

At the noise the husband rushed to help his wife, the light went out, and he found himself in the water. He started to cry, "Help!" The neighbors, hearing the noise, came downstairs to find out what was the matter, and when they got to their doors they could not go outside because of the water in the streets and in the houses. So they, too began to cry out, warning that there was a flood. The watchman, who was on dry ground, began to call out the guards;[24] hearing the noise, he alerted the chancellor and the priors, saying that at the gate of San Salvadore there were cries of "To arms! To arms!" And the priors exclaimed: "Listen a moment to what they are saying." To which the watchman replied: "They are shouting that enemy soldiers are inside." The priors responded by saying: "Ring, bellman, ring, to arms; Let them hang!" The bellman set about ringing the call to arms. The guards that were in the piazza grabbed their weapons and went to where each street entered the piazza, setting up chains and crying, "To arms, to arms." All the people, hearing the bell, came out of their houses armed, believing that Count Lutz was attacking; and when they got to the piazza, they found the guards positioned at the chained entrances to the piazza. The guards were shouting, "Who goes there? Who goes there?" Some were saying, "Viva Messer Ridolfo" and others were answering, "Friends, friends." There was so much noise that nobody could hear anyone else; the whole population was in the piazza in arms expecting the soldiers to arrive any moment, since many were saying that the enemy had got inside, and had reached a church called San Giorgio, which lies halfway between the city gate and the piazza.

The man responsible for this "romore" (literally "noise" but also "uproar") and for the general confusion, was the bellman, who by ringing the call to arms made the citizens agitated and confused "like drunken thrushes."[25] Being the bellman was not a simple job, though. At Florence no one had succeeded for seventeen years in ringing a full peal on "the great bell of the people of Florence," despite the fact that twelve men had tried pulling at once. Luckily in 1322 there arrived "a subtle master from Siena" who succeeded in doing so; in fact, with his "subtle and beautiful skill" two men were enough to make the bell move, and then just one to make it sound a full peal, notwithstanding its weight, "more than seventeen thousand pounds."[26]

Above all else, the bells established that the day was over: the *tintinabulum* (signal bell) at Città di Castello rang out each evening at the order of the senior magistrate "to remove any doubt as to whether it was still daytime or whether night had started . . . and after it had rung everyone knew that it was nighttime, and before everyone knew that it was still daytime."[27] The evening bell was supposed to strike three times over a sufficient interval that every citizen would be able to get back to his or her house from whatever part of the city they might be in at that moment; after the third had sounded, three more strikes were supposed to follow, and at that point no one could circulate through the city any more or be outside their house. Then, when the big bell of the commune sounded five hammerlike strokes, everyone had to cover the coals in their fireplace very carefully or else extinguish them altogether,[28] to prevent fires. But if a fire did occur there was another bell to let the city know, the one in the palazzo of the Podestà, rung at full peal.[29] Not that there was a lot they could do, even with the best will in the world: look at this miniature (fig. 42) showing Bern in flames. The piling of the ladders on top of one another, the smallness of

O man von der gebiet crifti zalt an
ccc. ii las Ist die ftatt Bern
aber verbrunnen von der crützgaffen
vntz an den ftalden damit anp fich aber
not vnd arbeit das arm lüte vnd arm mochten
gebuwen

Figure 42. *Bern in Flames.* Miniature, 1480–1485, from Diebold Schilling, *Spiezer Bilder Chronik.* Bern, Burgerbibliothek, MS Hist. Helv. I, 16, fol. 136.

Figure 43. *Santa Fina Stops a Fire.* Lorenzo di Niccolò di Pietro Gerini, detail from the *Pala di Santa Fina,* 1402. San Gimignano, Museo Civico.

the buckets, the few tubs, the frenetic disorganization of the men as they get in each other's way—all these foretell that the uncontrollable fire will win, even though there is a river nearby.[30] People had to count on the help of the saints, if they could get it, more than on human effort, as we see in a detail from the altar piece of Santa Fina, who subdues the flames that are destroying houses (fig. 43).

The language of the bells was precisely codified. For example, there were lugubrious peals that sounded if someone entered their final agony "so that the people, hearing that sound, should collect themselves in prayer."[31] If the dying person was a woman there were two peals; if it was a man, three; if it was a cleric, "as many as were the orders he had taken in life." Prayers, but also comments on the good points and bad points of the dying person, were no doubt mixed with thoughts of those surviving him or her. The thought of the imminent threshold of divine justice the dying person was about to cross, like everyone sooner or later, provoked emotion: the sense that city life was something shared did not cease, even in the moment at which one is most alone.

The final seconds of life were decisive, with a devil and an angel battling at the bedside of the dying person to seize their soul as it escaped from their mouth together with the last breath. "I am sorry he is not mine!" ("Doleo quia non est meus!") murmurs a defeated devil (at whom Saint Michael glares, his great wings outspread) as he sees that the balance is not shifting to his side, and that victory goes to Saint Peter, who has come down to "loosen," as he is empowered to do, the rope binding the wrists of a man lying supine on his deathbed, in a carved slab on the facade of the Church of San Pietro in Spoleto (fig. 44). So that believers should preserve a salutary dread of the fate that awaited them, the Evil One is the victor in the slab immediately below (fig. 45). Saint Michael now abandons the scene, and the balance shifts to the side of sin: the dying man's wrists are tightly bound by the rope and his hair is standing on end with fright; one devil is already seated astride him, and despite his desperate resistance a second one is dragging him off with evident glee. The inexorable sequel is seen at the far left: the infernal chasm[32] is swallowing up the damned soul, who has been pitched into it head first, so that the last thing we see of him is his flailing feet.[33]

When the canonical hours were rung by hand, nobody could have given a precise answer to the question, "What time is it?" But even when they were replaced by a great clock installed on the tower of the palazzo of the commune (at Siena this took place in 1359[34]), the division of the hours did not immediately become more regular, for the statutes continually mention the need to adjust the clock ("temperare l'oriolo") in order to try to get a grip on those hours, for they were always running too fast or too slow. The machinery might include automatons popping out on the hour to amuse the public, but at Brescia to this day the ones on the clock tower are called "i matti delle ore" ("the hourly crazies" or "the crazy timekeepers"). In 1460, the

Figures 44–45. *The Death of a Good Man and the Death of a Sinner.* Sculpture, last quarter of the twelfth century. Spoleto, Church of San Pietro.

statutes of Corciano still mention the obligation to "hire a master, who should take particular charge of the clock, and well and diligently care for it and adjust it."[35]

PIGS FOR GARBAGEMEN

Approaching the walls of a medieval city and entering it through a gate, we would immediately be struck by a barrage of contrasting odors, some of them decidedly unpleasant; we would hear the calls and cries of animals, the rumble of carts, the pounding of horses' hooves, the pealing of the bells, the voices of the people: noises and smells that would vary from one street or piazza to the next, and from working days to holidays.

People spent a lot of time out of doors, as we saw, because of the closeness of the houses and the workshops. Everyone knew everyone else, and they liked to chat while resting on the stone benches placed at the doors of the houses (fig. 40 above), eager to relish secrets told in hushed tones or piquant sallies. Sacchetti knew the custom well: "It was after dinner, and we were outside. Salvestro had a woman from Friuli like him, very agreeable, who was at the window that evening. As usual a number of the neighbors had gathered on the bench right outside the house, some of them stuffed with food, including I myself, the author. A discussion began. . . ."[36] Out of doors one listened to sermons, heard about the latest developments, took in performances by jugglers and trained animals, or watched as the guilty were punished, often in an atrocious manner.

To spread the news there were different categories of "voice professionals," first and foremost the heralds of the commune who rendered the resolutions of the town council operative by proclaiming them aloud: banishments of rebels and other unworthies who deserved exile, sentences and condemnations. The announcer (*banditore*) on horseback caught the attention of the folk by sounding a horn or trumpet.[37] Then there were the town messengers, who brought communications from the magistrates to individual citizens and would assume the task of carrying correspondence between private citizens, for a fee. There were no street addresses, so every time you sent a letter, you had to be sure to employ a carrier who knew his way around in the quarter where the recipient lived.[38] Then there were the "criers" (*gridatori*) and the common couriers: they were not public employees, but you could find them in the street or in the taverns, waiting for business—often men of miserable condition, living from hand to mouth, addicted to gaming and drinking. A popular work written early in the fourteenth century by the Dominican Jacopo da Cessole, *De ludis scacchorum* (On Games of chess), is a metaphor of the world and the social categories. Jacopo imagines the piece representing the ribalds and the gamblers as a man with "shaggy and dishevelled hair, in his right hand a few coins, in the left hand three dice; he uses a piece of rope for a belt, and from it hangs a bag full of

Figure 46. *A Letter Carrier Addicted to Gambling*. Miniature, 1458, from Jacopo da Cessole, *De ludis scacchorum*. Rome, Biblioteca Vaticana, MS Pal. Lat. 961, fol. 51v.

letters" (fig. 46). The exiguous amount of money and the "corda pro cingulo" (rope for a belt) are meant to recall how the vice of gaming leads to poverty and the temptation of theft. The dice evoke bad company and a sinful way of life, for those dedicated to gaming are cheats and frequenters of prostitutes, according to our Dominican. He has some advice for these gamblers-couriers and travelers: don't drink or eat to excess. When you arrive in an unfamiliar city, don't be too curious. Time is no longer the exclusive domain of the church, the gratuitous gift of God, but a precious resource of merchants,[39] which means that a letter that doesn't arrive on time can cause profits ("lucrum in mercatura") to be lost, or ruinous complications to arise.[40]

At Siena, right on the main piazza (piazza del Campo) beside the *barattería* (literally the "barratry," actually the public gaming house[41]) and the fish market, there was to be found the department of sanitation. Whoever tendered successfully for the corresponding excise duties also had the right to become an official crier. Let us read the public record for 9 October 1296: the competition to win the tender had been publicly announced by a town herald three times, on three different days, throughout the city. The highest bidder and thus the winner of the contract received from the commune of Siena the right for approximately a year to collect "all the garbage and manure and spilled cereal grains from piazza del Campo and the streets adjacent to it." He obtained as well, for the same period, "the right to cry [i.e., advertise] and put up for sale beasts of burden and horses," to give notice of lost objects, holidays, the creation of emergency governing commissions, the names of magistrates and doctors; and finally the right to keep, likewise in the piazza del Campo for the space of a year, "a sow and four piglets so that they can gather and eat all the spilled cereal."[42] This legal disposition immediately gives us a vivid idea of the state of the piazzas and streets through which passed, not without leaving steaming piles behind them, cows, horses, asses, mules, and flocks of sheep and goats; and in which hens and geese scratched for food. The pigs that functioned as sanitation workers while being fattened for free by rooting around in the refuse of the market place will in turn have left their own tangible memorials behind. These weren't the only pigs that ranged freely (fig. 47). The ones known as "porci di sant'Antonio" (Saint Anthony's swine) enjoyed the special privilege of being free to wander as they pleased through the city.[43] The devotion given to Saint Anthony was probably due to the fact that at the end of the eleventh century, in southern France, the relics of the saint, which had been brought there around half a century earlier, were credited with curing one of the numerous cases of ergotism. Ergotism, which results in convulsive symptoms, was called "sacred fire" or "Saint Anthony's fire," and is not to be confused with the disease today popularly called by the same name, which is actually *herpes zoster* or shingles. Ergotism was caused by the consumption of rye infected with the toxic fungus Claviceps purpurea (called *segale cornuta* or

"horned rye" in Italian).[44] Saint Anthony was also invoked against the plague, together with two other saints, Rocco, a plague victim himself, and Sebastian. The marks on the bodies of the sufferers recalled the numerous wounds on the body of Sebastian, who was condemned, at one point in his torment, to be shot full of arrows (fig. 48). His miraculous survival gave hope to those who were ill that by invoking this saint, they would be helped to resist the attack of the disease. The link between Saint Sebastian and the plague is also reinforced by the authority of Holy Scripture. Throughout the Middle Ages the spread of this epidemic was experienced as the unleashed ire of God, compared in the Psalms (7:13) to arrows released from a bow. In the Apocalypse (6:1–8) one of the four horsemen has a bow and arrows; together they bring the scourges of war, famine, pestilence, and death. The presence of Saints Anthony, Rocco, and Sebastian is an indicator to us that ergotism and plague had made their appearance in the place where the images were executed, enabling us to read out the history out the diseases that prevailed when the people of Europe lacked a medicine as potent as their faith.

"Saint Anthony's swine" animate two of the novellas of Sacchetti:

Figure 47. *A Flock of Sheep and a Pig Are Brought into Paris*. Miniature, 1317, from Yves, monk of Saint-Denis, *Vie et Martyre de Saint-Denis*. Paris, Bibliothèque Nationale, MS Fr. 2091, fol. 1.

Figure 48. *The Torture of Saint Sebastian*. Giovanni del Biondo, tempera panel, second half of the fourteenth century. Florence, Museo dell'Opera del Duomo. Scala / Art Resource, NY.

Anyone who knows Florence knows that on the first Sunday of every month there is an outing to San Gallo, where men and women go in company, for pleasure more than to seek pardon. Giotto set out one of these Sundays with his companions to go there, and when they were in via del Cocomero, where Giotto slowed to a virtual halt as he was telling a story, some of Saint Anthony's swine came along, and one of them, which was running furiously, raced between Giotto's legs, making him tumble to the ground. After struggling to his feet with the aid of his friends and shaking himself, he neither blamed the swine nor said a word in their direction, but turned to his companions half smiling and said, "Haven't they good reason? After all, I have gained thousands of lire in my day with their bristles, and I never gave them so much as a bowl of broth."[45]

A very different reaction came from a neighbor of Sacchetti, gouty and gluttonous, constrained to keep to his bed by illness but disinclined on that account to interrupt his habit of eating well. "It happened by chance that two swine of Saint Anthony, fine ones, came in almost every day by the street door, and then immediately went into" the room where the sick man was lying (evidently it was normal for them to make themselves at home, though surprising to us). The ailing glutton, even though a few of his friends advised him not to fool around with Saint Anthony, ordered a servant to take an axe and try to slaughter one of the pigs. There followed an indescribable commotion, because the wounded animals gored the servant and his gouty master; the screams and "yelps" actually brought the guards and their captain to the scene; and the strokes of their swords multiplied the quantity of blood flowing from various wounds, the howls, and the confusion. In the end the pigs got away, the servant almost lost a leg, and his master suffered for months and months and almost died. "Saint Anthony made this miracle, and so the saying goes: 'Fool around with *fanti* (servants), don't mess with *santi* [saints].'"[46]

Two more pigs running free in the streets of Florence during the plague of 1348 filled Boccaccio, an involuntary eyewitness to the spread of the epidemic, with horror: "My own eyes, as I said earlier, were witness to such a thing one day: when the rags of a poor man who died of this disease were thrown into the public street, two pigs came upon them, and, as they are wont to do, first with their snouts and then with their teeth they took the rags and shook them around; and within a short time,

after a number of convulsions, both pigs fell dead upon the ill-fated rags, as if they had been poisoned."[47]

Let us leave behind us the unaccustomed silence of this city of death, where the quantity of cadavers left in the houses and in the streets was so great that it was necessary to dig communal graves and fill them in layers, covering every layer with a little earth, "as though one were serving lasagna, with layers of cheese," wrote Marchionne di Coppo Stefani crudely (fig. 49).[48]

THE MARGINALIZED AND THE EXCLUDED

Even on an average day there were many striking things to see. Above all, the poor, with their filth and their disfigured bodies, their wounds, and the bad smell of someone forced to wander, with no way to change his clothing or refresh himself with a bath.[49] In the *Trionfo della Morte* (Triumph of death) in the Camposanto of Pisa, copied by Orcagna in the Church of Santa Croce in Florence (fig. 50), a compact group of mendicants are shown devastated by leprosy, or blind, or with their limbs amputated and shriveled, crying out their desperation through a scroll: "Since prosperity has left us / O Death, the medicine of every affliction / Come now and give us our last supper."[50]

Figure 49. *Burial of the Victims of the Plague at Tournai in 1349*. Miniature, fourteenth century, from Gilles le Muisit, *Annales*. Brussels, Koninklijke Bibliotheek Albert I, MS 13076–77, fol. 24v. Photo: Royal Library of Belgium.

Figure 50. *The Poor and Afflicted Cry Out for Death*. Andrea Orcagna, detail from *The Triumph of Death*, fresco, middle of the fourteenth century. Florence, Museo di Santa Croce.

In the fresco in Pisa, painted by Buffalmacco between roughly 1336 and 1342, as in the one in Florence, the poor, being old and ill, wish to pass over to the next world, not because of Christian thoughts or anxiety about reaching heaven but only because they cannot enjoy the sort of life that the wealthy have. Their entreaty ends within the limits of the purely human: they want one last banquet, but they ask for it with a blasphemous play on words that derides the sacrament of the Eucharist (the Last Supper).

It was easy to become or to be poor: a bad harvest was enough, or an illness, or the death of a husband or a father; peasants, wageworkers, single persons, ill persons, frequently became poor. All it took was failure to pay back a sum of money on time, an uprising, a house fire, a broken arm, to go to ruin: that's right, just a simple fracture—there were no X-rays and plaster casts back then!—and one found oneself enrolled in the category of the crippled, unable to work and begging for charity. Divine intervention would have had to be continuous to avoid the tragic consequences of accidents in the workplace (fig. 51). A mason who fell but remained clinging to the wall by his fingernails was luckily aided by angels who braced his feet "for the better part of the day": that was how long it took until his companions arrived to

Figure 51. *Santa Fina Saves a Carpenter Who Is Falling from a Scaffold.* Lorenzo di Niccolò di Pietro Gerini, detail from the *Pala di Santa Fina,* 1402. San Gimignano, Museo Civico. Scala / Art Resource, NY.

Figure 52. *A Mason Hanging by His Fingertips Is Miraculously Saved by Angels.* Miniature, 1281–1284, from Alfonso X the Wise, *Cantigas de Santa María.* Florence, Biblioteca Nazionale Centrale, MS B. R. 20, fol. 88r.

Figure 53. *Saint Francis Cures the Demoniacs.* Bonaventura Berlinghieri, detail from an altarpiece depicting the *Miracles performed by Saint Francis in life and after death,* panel, 1235. Pescia, Church of San Francesco.

relieve him (fig. 52).[51] The poor comprised the deranged and the insane, too, lumped together for short as the *indemoniati* (i.e., those possessed by devils) and compelled to swell the ranks of a sordid and ragged crowd (fig. 53). The church enjoined help for the indigent but without any examination of the social causes or desire to rectify them; quite the contrary, in fact, for the church justified the existence of the poor man as the necessary instrument for the salvation of the rich one, whose many sins could only be wiped out by seizing the opportunity to do good works. Listen to Giordano da Pisa preaching to a devout and approving crowd:

> Why does God make so much diversity in the world, the rich, the poor, the strong, the
> weak? Because he has all in his care: for if all were kings, who would bake the bread?

Who would work the soil? God has ordained that there shall be rich and poor so that the rich may be served by the poor, and the poor succored by the rich, and this regimen is common to all peoples. To what end are the poor ordained? To enable the rich to gain eternal life through them.[52]

The same preacher used a brilliant, mollifying metaphor to explain:

Feed wood to a fire and it grows; and the more you add, the bigger it gets. Just so, in a spiritual sense the poor, the miserable, the afflicted, the needy, are the firewood; and the fire is the love and the pity of the saintly man who sees the misery of his neighbor and is moved to compassion, and does them good deeds in the way we said. In this way his own good increases because of the evil of suffering in the world, just as the fire increases by being fed wood. . . . So you see how necessary the poor and the afflicted are! If God had not created such evils, then all these goods, that are so numerous and so good, would not exist. If there were no poor, there would be no one to give alms, or compassion, or the virtue of pity.[53]

The Church urged charity, using the shining example of the saints. The episodes of the legend of the martyr San Lorenzo (Saint Lawrence) refer historically to the fourth century, but the medieval painters embed them in an urban setting contemporary with themselves. In two scenes from the life of the martyr (figs. 54–55), painted by Ambrogio di Baldese around 1380 (Lorenzo distributes the treasures of his church to the poor; Lorenzo in prison baptizes the jailer and cures the infirm), we see that only the saint is dressed in the manner of the ancient world, with an ample toga draped over his shoulders. For everything else, the painter has depicted things he will have seen countless times with his own eyes: among the poor there is an old woman, and a young one with her baby; the infirm overlap with the beggars in the usual array of blind and crippled persons. Behind the shoulders of San Lorenzo in the act of giving, there is a man in fourteenth-century dress who appears not to share the same generous impulse as the saint.

Pity toward the indigent and the marginalized was precariously balanced and could easily be transformed into indifference, or worse, into open conflict, should the numbers of persons in difficulty suddenly rise and the community prove unable to sustain the burden. "Babies abandoned in destitution by their mothers will be taken in, but not all, so as not to create an incentive for mothers deliberately to expose their children. The superior will decide according to his best judgment," say the statutes of the Hospital of Saint John in Brussels in 1211. "If all the illegitimate children were taken in indiscriminately, it could happen that there would be such a quantity that the hospitals would not be able either to care for them or to bear the strain, given that many would abandon them; such persons would become very

Figure 54. *San Lorenzo Distrib-utes the Treasures of His Church to the Poor.* Ambrogio di Baldese, detail from *Scenes from the Life of San Lorenzo,* panel, c. 1380. Avignon, Musée du Petit Palais.

Figure 55. *San Lorenzo in Prison Baptizes the Jailer and Cures the Infirm.* Ambrogio di Baldese, detail from *Scenes from the Life of San Lorenzo,* panel, c. 1380. Avignon, Musée du Petit Palais.

much more inclined to sin if they knew that in any case their babies would be cared for, and consequently they would feel themselves absolved of the greatest respon-sibilities and worries": these emphatic words come from King Charles VII (1403–1461), addressing him-self to the Hospital of the Holy Spirit of Paris.[54] At Florence those who wanted to abandon their babies yet offer them a slim chance of survival, took them to a place beneath the Loggia del Bigallo. The Capitani della Misericordia (Captains of Compassion), whose office was located there, would take the little ones in and put them on public view in the hope of finding women disposed to act as mothers who would accept them. A large portion of a fresco painted in 1386 by Niccolò di Pietro Gerini and Ambrogio di Baldese on the external facade of this edifice is still preserved, and it depicts this charitable practice in a highly optimistic vein (fig. 56).[55]

Figure 56. *The Captains of Compassion Hand Abandoned Children over to Foster Mothers.* Niccolò di Pietro Gerini and Ambrogio di Baldese, fresco (fragmentary), 1386. Florence, Museo del Bigallo.

Charity tended to melt away, or even evaporate altogether, during the frequent famines that upset the social equilibrium. At Siena for example, in 1329, after the Nine decided not to maintain the poor of the city any longer with distributions of food, violent tumults erupted.

Those poor, who were numberless, made a desperate decision: they ran to the major palazzo,[56] from which these orders had previously issued, and when they got there, some began to cry out, "Pity!"; others cried out, "Burn it down!"; and yet others, "Die!" This was all going on at the same time, and such a noise arose that the whole city was galvanized, with everyone seizing whatever arms were at hand to protect themselves. Armed troops emerged from the palazzo intending to confront this tumult of the poor, but they were ineffective; indeed, the poor actually set about doing what the armed troops who had come out only declared their intent to do: striking hard with stones and clubs, they assaulted that palace, and chased the troops, who probably feared coming to much worse harm, back inside.[57]

After the uprising was eventually brought under control, harsh repression followed, with arrests, banishments, torture, hangings, and finally the decision to drive

Figure 57. *The Poor Are Driven Out of Siena.* Miniature, first half of the fourteenth century, from *Il Libro del Biadaiolo.* Florence, Biblioteca Laurenziana, MS Tempi 3, fol. 57v.

Figure 58. *San Francesco Cures the Lepers.* Detail from the Tavola Bardi, *Miracles Performed by San Francesco in Life and After Death,* panel, second quarter of the thirteenth century. Florence, Santa Croce, Cappella Bardi.

all the poor outside the walls of the city. In the *Libro del Biadaiolo* (Book of the Grain Merchant), from which this passage is taken, the account of the expulsion—which was preceded, as was the custom, by the sound of a trumpet, and which became operative three days after being officially announced—is faithfully mirrored in the corresponding miniature (fig. 57). "And all the guards went striking the poor hard with staffs and stones, and driving them out of the gate, with no regard whether they were children or adults, women or men, pregnant or not pregnant."[58]

Then there were the lepers, permanently excluded from the cities and forced to shake a particular kind of castanet or little bell wherever they went so that everyone else would have time to move off and not to have to look at their devastated faces or smell the stench of their wounds. That is the reason San Francesco (Saint Francis of Assisi) begins his *Testamento* by recalling his encounter with the lepers, the moment at which his life changed radically: "The Lord granted me, brother Francesco, to commence to do penitence thus, for since I was still in sin, to look upon the lepers seemed to me too bitter a thing; and the Lord himself brought me among them, and I used them with mercy. And as I went away from them, that which seemed bitter to me was changed in me into a sweetness of soul and of body. After that I hesitated for a little, and then I left the world behind" (fig. 58).[59]

The aspect of the lepers was particularly loathsome, but the horror they aroused was increased by the fact that it was commonly held that their disease was a divine punishment for sins they had committed. Sacchetti, for example, is very well pleased to be able to conclude that a friar who was a "hypocrite, more of a rascal than a religious" had been justly punished with the disease: "He became leprous to such a degree that he had to abandon both the order [of San Francesco] and this earth. He lived for a number of years with such a putrid infirmity, and then died the death he deserved. And it was one of the miracles done by our Lord that this hypocritical and vicious friar, who made a show of being a man of saintly life under the cover of the Franciscan habit, had to display his defect on the outside, through the disease of leprosy, which was inside the cover of his body."[60]

THE GRIM TONE OF LIFE

Another baleful spectacle was the public punishment of convicted criminals: exposed, in the best of cases, to the derision and insults of the bystanders, they were frequently condemned to very harsh penalties, like the ones prescribed for adulterers (fig. 59). In the worst cases they were atrociously tortured even as they were being taken to their deaths, so that their screams and spasms would be stamped firmly into the minds of the citizens—a pointed warning to mend one's ways. The sodomites were burned at the stake; the thieves were whipped, taken to the stocks, branded on the cheek with a red-hot iron, then forced to stay there for hours;[61] the blasphemers were whipped and then dragged through the city with pincers that gripped their tongues;[62] the murderers were tied to the tail of an ass or a horse,

Figure 59. *The Punishment of the Adulterers.* Miniature, twelfth century. Agen, Bibliothèque Municipale, MS 42, fol. 42v.

dragged through the whole city, and finally hung,[63] as were the traitors and the disturbers of the public peace: in this case, to prolong the torment, they were suspended upside down.[64]

Wars, but also low-intensity conflicts, were continual; to the Franciscans who greeted him with "God give you peace!" John Hawkwood, the celebrated mercenary captain, answered, "What kind of greeting is it to come to me and say, may God make me die of hunger? Do you not know that I live by war, and that peace would undo me?"[65] Wars and conflicts left behind them long trains of hatred and vengeance, harshening the souls of the folk and habituating them to the violence of everyday life. For example, the Consiglio della Campana (the supreme council in Siena) on 30 August 1255 discussed at length the methods of punishment to be used against the castle of Torniella in Val di Merse, which had rebelled against Siena. All agreed that the place itself should be leveled to the ground, but how to punish the inhabitants? Some wanted to blind them, others to deprive them each of just one eye; some to cut off their hands and feet, others to cut off just one hand and foot; and some to make an end of it and hang them all.[66] Still at Siena, in 1338 Agniolo di Ghino del Favilla endured a horrific punishment for having set fire to the San Marco gate, at the instigation of the Florentines: "He was taken and fixed to a cart with red-hot clamps; his hands were burned off at the said gate; and then he was torn into four pieces and placed at four gates; they put one quarter of him at each gate."[67]

A vast assortment of such cruelties could be put on exhibit, but I shall forbear; the representation, terribly expressive, of the last voyage of the captain of Brescia, Tebaldo Brusato, who had rebelled against the emperor Henry VII in 1311,[68] can stand for the rest (fig. 60). I do however wish to compare the torment of Tebaldo with that inflicted on someone who made a saint (in this case Saint Eligius) angry—for a little relief, since here the culprit is a devil, and his anguish will distress no one. The scene was painted by Lorenzo di Niccolò di Pietro Gerini on a predella around 1390 (fig. 61). Eligius, who lived in the seventh century, had been an able smith before he became a bishop, and our painter, as usual, shows us a medieval workshop. Various implements and horseshoes are suspended on the wall (iron was such a valued commodity in the Middle Ages that horseshoes could even be used as decorative elements on the doors of a church, as at Chablis in France; fig. 62). The bellows blowing oxygen into the fire is activated by a lever, and the saint, wearing a fresh apron and holding his hammer in one hand, is bending over his anvil. Other surprising details are visible, however, taken from two episodes in the life of Eligius. To shoe a restless horse one day, the saintly smith sheared the animal's foreleg off, placed the detached limb on the anvil so that he could work on it easily, and when the hoof was shod, reattached it to the beast. The leg miraculously became whole again, without the horse feeling any pain. During his daily routine, however, kicks from horses were not the only thing Eligius had to dodge, for the devil also came to torment him relentlessly, disguised as a beautiful girl, though in the fresco her claws and her batlike wings give her away. Patience was not apparently one of the saint's virtues, and one day, tired of bearing so much provocation, he seized a pair of red-hot tongs and used them to squeeze the nose of the temptress (in fig. 61 they look like a pair of rods or sticks in front of her face). Many a viewer would have been present when the same punishment was applied in real life to malefactors like Tebaldo Brusato (in fig. 60, the hot pincers gripping his nose are clearly visible). Here the viewer could take pleasure in seeing it applied to the Devil himself, the same devil who on the frescoed walls of the churches was always busy inflicting a varied repertoire of torments on the damned—perhaps my own future companions in agony, the terrified viewer must have thought to himself.

PUNISHMENT IN THE HEREAFTER

When we gaze on an image of *Inferno* (Hell) today, with the damned hung by their genitals, forced to swallow molten lead, impaled, sawed apart, spitted and torn to pieces, we certainly find it striking, but for us these events are happening in an un-real place, and we think of them as the fruits of the imaginative power of the painter and the church that commissioned him. The reaction of a contemporary of Giotto, however, who paused before the *Giudizio Universale* (Last Judgment) in the Scrovegni chapel in Padua, would have been much more profound and violent: he was looking at a likeness of a reality he knew, through living in the city or through stories told by neighbors and relatives. But that reality was presented to him as projected into a time without end, a time just as true as the time he had lived through for a viewer accustomed to frame every action within the religious setting of the divine will. So painted images could be an extraordinarily aggressive medium in the Middle Ages. Terror mounted at the thought that physical pain, unbearable but finite because ending with death, would continue in the underworld forever, without end.

   "O sinner who in this life abides/you are wrapped up in worldly cares/Fix your mind on these harsh figures/Who in this dark inferno bear their woe/*Exactly as they are so will you be*/If you do not repent of the evil you have done,"[69] declares a scroll, one of many that provide a running commentary on the fresco of *Inferno* by Buffal-macco in the Camposanto of Pisa. Hell is here represented for the first time as an autonomous theme, detached from the *Giudizio Universale*.[70]

   So that the impact of the images on the Pisans would be lasting and beneficial, epigraphs were added in rhyming verse to facilitate recall: they served both as memory aids and lecture notes for those who had heard the sermons, and everyone could carry the message of that extraordinary and imposing painted homily back home with them, and indeed would remember it for the rest of their lives. From the

Figure 60. *The Execution of Tebaldo Brusato during the Siege of Brescia in 1311*. Miniature, 1340–c. 1350, from the *Codex Balduini Trevirensis*. Koblenz, Landeshauptarchiv, 1C1, fol. 13r.

Figure 61. *The Devil Tempts Saint Eligius at Work*. Lorenzo di Niccolò di Pietro Gerini, detail from *Scenes from the Life of Saint Eligius,* panel, c. 1390. Avignon, Musée du Petit Palais.

Figure 62. Door decorated with iron horseshoes, fourteenth century. Chablis, Church of Saint-Martin.

Figure 63. *A Woman in Hell, Wearing a Serpent-tailed Gown.* Andrea Orcagna, detail from *Inferno* (Hell), fresco, middle of the fourteenth century. Florence, Museo di Santa Croce. Scala/Art Resource, NY.

pulpits, the Dominicans and Franciscans thundered in fiery language, their words often inspired by the very same frescoes; thus the fears of viewers were fused into a tight circle. San Bernardino, for example, exclaimed in 1424 in the Church of Santa Croce in Florence: "And you, woman, wearing a flowing gown with a serpent's tail, as Merlin prophesied that the time would come when women would wear the tails of serpents, and then we would be in great danger, I tell you that to me it seems that that time has begun. . . . And you, husband, you are the reason that the woman assumes this tail, and the tailor has a hand in it, too, and so does the seller of cloths, if he does it for the purpose of fashioning a tail, and the woman who wears it—all are sinning mortally." An audience of husbands and wives will have glanced with a shiver at the *Inferno* painted in the very same church by Andrea Orcagna, in which a damned woman with a long serpent-tailed gown wrings her hands in desperation, at the mercy of a soldier armed with a long dagger (fig. 63).[71]

The power of images was not confined to the ambit of religious faith: from the second half of the thirteenth century, traitors and forgers who were condemned in absentia began to be depicted in the act of being burned or, more often, hung head down. This was even done on the walls of the most important public buildings, and epigraphs were furnished indicating the name of the criminal and heaping insults on him. Such "defamatory painting" (*pittura infamante*)[72] was a particularly effective form of punishment, because it implicated in his shame all the persons with whom the pictorially condemned individual had any relationship and exposed them to the disapproval of others as well. A final array of examples will drive home my point about the pervasive interplay in the Middle Ages between daily reality and the painted image, both religious and secular: we have the sequence of men and women who have been hanged, some of them upside down, in Giotto's *Inferno* in the Scrovegni Chapel at Padua (fig. 64), the many examples of individuals hung in effigy for the purpose of defaming them (fig. 65), and a group of women with their babies hung from the handles of carts in a horrid act of vengeance perpetrated in wartime (fig. 66).

Figure 64. *The Punishment (Here, by Hanging) of the Damned in Hell*. Giotto, detail from the *Last Judgment*, fresco, beginning of the fourteenth century. Padua, Cappella Scrovegni.

Figure 65. *A Military Commander Defamed Pictorially.* Andrea del Sarto, drawing based on fourteenth-century iconography, 1530. Florence, Galleria degli Uffizi, Andrea del Sarto, *Disegni,* fol. 330f.

Figure 66. *Women and Babies Hung from the Handles of Carts.* Miniature, fifteenth century, from *L'Histoire ancienne depuis la Création* and *Faits des Romains.* Paris, Bibliothèque Nationale, MS Fr. 250, fol. 215.

LESSONS AND COMPUNCTION

Many ideas were inspired by things that went on out of doors, which was just as much the case in the cities as it was in the countryside. The sermons of renowned preachers like Bernardino of Siena, for example, whom we have seen preaching in

Santa Croce, were heard in the open because he was so famous during his lifetime that there were hardly any churches capacious enough to hold the crowds who wanted to hear him.[73] Men and women were separated by a cloth partition so that they would not distract each other with sidelong glances, and in unison they fixed their attention on the man in the temporary pulpit. Sano di Pietro, in a panel painting formerly in the hall of the cathedral chapter of Siena, represents Bernardino thus, preaching in 1427 in front of the unfinished Church of San Francesco to a rapt public, the men separated from the women by the usual cloth partition and all of them hunched on the ground (fig. 67).[74] The painting was made while the saint was still alive—there is no halo, the attribute of sanctity, around his head—and is a visual testament to a devotion and a popularity that were already very great. The door of the church is open, to suggest the overflowing crowd, which the edifice is unable to contain. Long serpent-tailed gowns were not the only thing that Bernardino prohibited: "Singing about the chivalrous knights on days officially set apart as holy days, above all, during Lent, is a mortal sin on the part of the singer and of whoever attends to listen to him, and likewise on the part of whoever gives him any aid or favor or could prevent him from singing and doesn't; for all of them it is a mortal sin."[75] The reference is precious evidence because it immediately evokes occasions for assembly, social intercourse, diversion, and instruction of a kind that has now entirely disappeared. It was not just the thrilling stories of the knights and their adventures that were sung, but also the stories of the saints: for example, the life of Saint Aibertus (early twelfth century) recounts how as a youth, when he was still living in his father's house but already "a lover of sanctity, by chance one day he had heard a performer who narrated in song the life and the conversion of Saint Theobald, and the hard life of penitence he led." That sung performance helped to push Aibertus toward the ascetic life.[76]

Games of sleight of hand, trained animals, and songs and little concerts were habitual spectacles, especially when the arrival of one of the religious holidays made it likely that a numerous public would turn up for these tempting attractions.[77] Franco Sacchetti must have been an alert observer of the professional tricksters who always succeeded in duping the simple "coarse" people with their nimble fingers, and *gherminella,* the name of one of these games, is still a synonym for "deceptive trick" even today.

Passera della Gherminella was virtually a swindler, always going about torn and frayed and with a cap on his head; most of the time he carried a stick in his hand like it was the rod of office of a Podestà, and about two braccia of rope, as though to spin a top. The *gherminella* trick worked like this: he held the stick in his two hands and put the cord on it, giving it a few twists. When a coarse fellow came along, Passera would say, "Which is inside, which is outside?" and he always had some silver coins in his hand so

that he could offer to bet. The coarse fellow, seeing the way the cord was and thinking that he could pull it out, would say, "The cord is on the outside," and Passera would say, "It is inside." The fellow would pull on the cord, but no matter what he did, the cord would either be inside or outside, whichever way Passera chose. Often he deliberately lost a round in order to tempt people to make a bigger bet. When he had burned practically every man around with this trick, especially at the corner of the Marignolli house where they sell straw [in the modern via de' Cerretani], one day a guy who sometimes took part in this trick with him in the tavern, said to him, "Passera, I've been thinking, if you were to go to Lombardy, the people there are so thick you could win as much as you liked, especially at Como and Bergamo. The men there are so thick they are like rams. If you want I will come with you."[78]

The trip to Bologna, Ferrara, Piacenza, Lodi, Milan, Como, Bergamo, Brescia, Verona, Mantua, and Padua was a fiasco, because the people there turned out to be sharp and didn't take the bait. The prestidigitator returned to Florence, where he had the same success as always—a caustic conclusion to the novella, with which Sacchetti hoped to shame his fellow Florentines.

FORBIDDEN GAMES

Another much-loved game, but a dangerous one for the public peace and morality, was the game of dice.[79] Heated with wine (figs. 68–69) and with gaming, with the excitement of winning and losing, often ruinously,[80] men abandoned themselves to cursing and were quick to throw punches, with brawls and wounds as the result. And if a woman were to take part, disapproval was transformed into open and fierce condemnation, something we can observe in a canticle of Alfonso X the Wise, and the corresponding illuminated page (fig. 70):[81] in Puglia there was a very beautiful church with a finely carved portal, and the Virgin on her throne with the Child, flanked by two angels, in the lunette. The angels had one hand to their breasts, which signified "their total and fervid submission to the divine will"; in the other hand each held "books of great value," which indicated "their universal wisdom." During a feast of the Madonna a company of gamblers and cheats, together with a "licentious German woman," began to play at dice right in front of the church.[82] The woman lost, and in a fury "committed a transgression," heaping insults on the Madonna and hurling a stone at her, which was providentially knocked aside by the hand of one of the two angels, who from that moment on remained with his hand open in a gesture of defense. The bystanders grabbed the woman, tied her up, and threw her onto a fire to burn. The illuminator has followed the narrative closely in every detail, including

Figure 67. *San Bernardino Preaching in Front of the Church of San Francesco at Siena.* Sano di Pietro, panel, 1427. Hall of the cathedral chapter, Siena. Scala / Art Resource, N.Y.

Figure 68. *Drinkers at a Tavern.* Miniature, fifteenth century, from the *Tacuinum Sanitatis.* Paris, Bibliothèque Nationale, MS Lat. 9333, fol. 85.

Figure 69. *A Brawl in a Tavern.* Fresco, beginning of the fifteenth century, from a lost cycle by Giotto. Padua, Palazzo della Ragione.

Figure 70. *The Death of the Woman Who Had Insulted the Virgin While Playing at Dice.* Miniature, 1281–1284, from Alfonso X the Wise, *Cantigas de Santa María.* Florence, Biblioteca Nazionale Centrale, MS B. R. 20, fol. 20r.

the angel's intervening hand. The last scene shifts away from the church to show the place where the burning is carried out. The culprit has already collapsed on the ground amid the flames, observed by two rows of satisfied executioners. So that the warning may create a greater sense of identification in viewers, three citizens, two women and a man, observe the act of torture from windows opportunely located in an upper story.

Over the centuries, public authorities and preachers vacillated in their view of games of chance, which they held to be illicit, but also, from time to time, justifiable, and even useful if regulated in a *baratteria,* a gaming house, by the authorities, because of the economic benefit to the city treasury.[83]

There were prohibitions, just as wobbly, in the city statutes, against *battagliole,* simulated battles using fists, wooden weapons, and stones in which adolescents regularly took part. These *battagliole* often got out of hand and turned from contests for fun into bloody "rumbles" that involved the whole city, adolescents and adults,[84] in the use of knives, lead balls, and clubs. Despite injury and death, the authorities limited themselves for a long time to containing the excesses, case by case, because the *battagliole* were of too much use as training for real war. In the fourteenth century, however, because of the ever more frequent employment of mercenary troops, the *battagliole* declined in importance to the point of becoming useless. At that point, they were firmly condemned by those in government as dangerous pretexts for revolt and sedition and by the preachers as a pure exercise of violence.[85]

PERMITTED SPECTACLES

Opportunities for more peaceful encounters and diversions came from jugglers and tumblers, strolling players, and minstrels. Numberless sanctions and prohibitions against games and spectacles in the open testify to the habitual presence of mimes, acrobats, and musicians, male and female, at the theater, at marriage feasts, in churchs, during processions, in and near cemeteries.[86] The custom was so common and familiar that we aren't surprised to find these entertainers frozen in bas-relief on the stone walls of churches. They invade manuscripts, too, adorning the initial letters of the sacred texts or, more freely, the margins of the columns of script: a moment of pause and distraction for the monk or the laic at prayer, as he followed with his gaze the exhibitions of the dancers, musicians, acrobats, and wild animal tamers. Who knows where the thoughts of Geoffrey Luttrell wandered as he read the *Psalter* (a collection of psalms and other prayers) he had commissioned and his eyes inevitably fell on the attractive miniatures that accompany the sacred text? How was he supposed to think of God and his own sins while smiling at the elegant girl dancing on the shoulders of her companion (fig. 71), or the strolling player on stilts (fig.

72), or the one dressed up as a bishop who is making a hare jump through a hoop (fig. 73)?

Figure 71. *A Girl Dancing on the Shoulders of Her Companion.* Miniature, beginning of the fourteenth century. London, British Library, Luttrell Psalter, fol. 68. By Permission of the British Library.

Figure 72. *Strolling Player on Stilts.* Miniature, beginning of the fourteenth century. London, British Library, Luttrell Psalter, fol. 70v. By Permission of the British Library.

Figure 73. *Strolling Player Making a Hare Jump Through a Hoop.* Miniature, beginning of the fourteenth century. London, British Library, Luttrell Psalter, fol. 84. By Permission of the British Library.

Sometimes the illustrator amuses himself by making a joke at the expense of exaggerated claims, as in this miniature (fig. 74) in which the artist draws (with a smile) the efforts of a trainer who thinks he can teach a bear to talk by shouting "A, B, C" at it. The bear responds with nothing but "A," the single letter no doubt representing something a lot closer to an animal grunt than a human vocalization.

The strolling players were naturally able to recite difficult texts, whether sacred dramas or worldly stories. In the illuminated frontispiece of the *Térence des ducs* (1415) we find represented a medieval version of an antique stage show, anachronistic but very instructive for our purposes (fig. 75). A stage labeled "theatrum" appears in the foreground, with *joculatores* (players) wearing masks—one of them a mask of a skull—and playing their parts with expressive gestures. In the center, in a little theater for marionettes labeled "scena," an actor reads from a book that he holds in his hands; and all around him are the spectators, labeled "populus Romanus."[87]

Even a funeral could have the appearance of a sort of spectacle. Niccolò degli Alberti, buried in the Church of Santa Croce at Florence in 1377, "had a great honor of flags, covered horses, men in their finest costumes and women and servants and

Figure 74. *A Trainer Tries to Teach a Bear to Talk.* Miniature, 1120, from the *Commentaries of Saint Jerome.* Cambridge, Trinity College, MS O.4.7, fol. 75r.

Figure 75. *A Theatrical Show.* Miniature, 1415, from the *Térence des Ducs.* Paris, Bibliothèque de l'Arsenal, MS 664, fol. IV.

the poor and many large candles and many other extremely beautiful ornaments at the casket, and an infinite quantity of large candles on the tomb in the church," wrote Marchionne di Coppo Stefani in his *Cronaca fiorentina,* for example.[88]

The passing was first announced by one or more "criers of the dead" on horseback; a great banquet in the house in mourning followed, and then the funeral rite, which was also very expensive. Naturally the costs and the number of persons involved varied in relation to the wealth of the family of the deceased.

Let us look at a concrete case: whom do we find on the list of those who received compensation for the exequies of a "barlettaio" (a maker of barrels) named Masino in Siena in 1291?[89] Barbers, shoemakers, and tailors had busied themselves so as to present the deceased in an impeccable manner, freshly shaved and wearing a new suit from head to foot, including a bonnet and soled leggings. The cloth merchant, the tailor, the old clothes dealer, and others took care of the veil and the kerchief of the widow, and of her suit, sewn of brown cloth. On the other hand, the accoutrements for the funeral, covers, palls, and cushions, were rented from a sort of funeral supply service. The vigil over the corpse cost a good number of candles, large and small, and many more were consumed on the day of the funeral during the ceremony, including the mass. Then there was recompense for the children who had walked in single file with large candles in their hands, for the men who had transported the coffin (which had also cost a pretty penny), for those who had dug the grave, and for the criers of the dead on horseback. For the exequies in church the friars were rewarded with a hundred loaves, a barrel of wine, and a hundred fish— carp, to be precise. The baker and the butcher furnished a further forty-two loaves and enough mutton from castrated sheep for the large meal consumed by relatives and visitors in the house of Masino on the day of the funeral. Finally, for the peace of his soul, the priest of San Vigilio, the clergy and the nuns of the Abbey of San Donato, the priest of San Pietro all'Ovile, the priest and the clergy of Sant'Antonio, were all mobilized to provide prayer vigils and masses; and all were adequately compensated.

HUMAN MEDICINE

Whether or not Masino received any medical care (not that it did any good), and if so from whom, we do not know. To consult a doctor was very expensive; but the diagnosis, cloaked in lofty language that was often incomprehensible to the patient and his family, had little influence on the course of the disease. The study of medicine was not built around the direct observation of the human body, but instead on books: the first human dissections were carried out at Bologna at the end of the thirteenth century, but only the anatomists of the Renaissance would really alter the inherited conceptions of the Middle Ages. Medical doctors were grounded in what remained of ancient knowledge, which was mostly known through misleading translations and adaptations. They let themselves be guided by etymologies that were pure constructs but that were immediately reassuring, and by the teleological principle that assigned every organ a function within the context of an all-embracing theological system: a woman's body, for example, is formed for the sole purpose of procreation because that is what the book of Genesis says. Doctors did not so much describe the organs of the female body as "project" them, using a lot of imagination and following preconstituted mental models, to demonstrate that all of them corresponded perfectly to the unique end assigned to woman by the Creator.[90]

The garb that doctors wore was red in color, costly (because the pigment used was extremely expensive), and trimmed with vair, a highly prized fur.[91] These were the normal distinguishing marks of a doctor, and immediately made his professional identity clear. Two procedures were enough for him to make a diagnosis: feeling the sick person's pulse and examining their urine against the light (fig. 76). The urine was collected in a specially made elongated container, which the patient's relatives undertook to bring to the doctor in a characteristic cylindrical basket before deciding to request an expensive medical visit at home. Franco Sacchetti often likes to make doctors the subjects of caricature: he is particularly ferocious in his

Figure 76. *A Doctor Feels the Pulse of a Patient and Scrutinizes His Urine.* From a collection of medical treatises; end of the thirteenth century. Avignon, Bibliothèque Municipal, MS 1019, fol. 86v.

description of Maestro Gabbadeo (literally "Master Cheat-God") from Prato, poor and badly dressed ("he always wore a very high hood, which had a short tip at the side big enough to hold half a bushel of grain, and two flaps at the front that looked like two lumps of smoked pork"[92]). Gabbadeo was deluded by a friend, who persuaded him to leave Prato and come to practice in Florence as a way to escape from *mendicume* (indigence), although in order to cut a decent figure in the big city he would need a nicely decked-out horse, a servant, and a new outfit. To save money Gabbadeo bought a colt, and his wife eagerly removed "the trim and the muffs of vair" from her own finest dress and used them to replace the worn-out flaps of her husband's headgear. When he reached Florence Gabbadeo took up a station close to a spice and drug vendor in the Mercato Vecchio. "And when he had waited there for a while on horseback, a container of urine was put in his hand which came from a woman who lived in Torcicoda [a street near Santa Croce] who had become his patient." The colt, however, caught sight of a "porter carrying a pig on his head," took fright, began to snort, and tried to get away. The doctor quickly lost control of his mount, but not his grip on the container of urine:

> but the urine was spraying this way and that, and all of it went on his bonnet and his face and his clothing, and a few splashes went into his mouth; and despite all that he never let go. The horse ran through the stalls of the dealers in secondhand hardware, with the doctor holding the urine container in his hand, and in one dealer's shop there were a number of graters and ladles and pans and fire chains [used for hanging cauldrons over the fireplace]. The horse crashed into these appliances, causing all of them to fall; and the tip of the doctor's hood got caught in a fire chain, so that the hood, along with all its vair, of which there was plenty, remained stuck there. And the doctor, bareheaded now but still on the horse, which was running harder than ever because of the clatter of the falling iron, never lost his grip on the urine container, while the horse went racing down past the house of the Tornaquinci, and further on toward the gate leading to Prato, with the doctor completely unable to rein him in.[93]

It was the toll collectors who succeeded in bringing this chase to a halt by closing the city gate. After explaining what had occurred, the victim, too ashamed to be seen in such a filthy condition and with his head uncovered, stayed in their hut until dark. But in the long run he did return to his practice, because there was a shortage of doctors in Florence. "Knowing little, sitting on his old nag inspecting the fluid in urine containers without spilling it on himself, he saved no less than six hundred florins in a few years; and then he died, and in his coffin he bore his book on his body, as though he were Hippocrates or Galen."[94]

Corpses lie in heaps, cut down by the scythe of Death, who soars above them, in the *Trionfo della Morte* (Triumph of Death) painted by Buffalmacco in the Camposanto of Pisa (fig. 77); one of the dead is a doctor, shown with a characteristic elongated container of urine in his hand and a book to represent his formal learning (fig. 78). In the *Tebaide* (Thebiad), another part of the same fresco cycle, the painter has shown a failed attempt by a devil to disguise himself as a doctor; a scroll, which has vanished today, read: "The venerable abbot Macarius, of holy life and great devotion,

Figure 77. *A Heap of Corpses Cut Down by Death Includes a Doctor.* Buffalmacco, detail from *Trionfo della Morte* (Triumph of Death), fresco, c. 1343. Pisa, Camposanto. Scala / Art Resource, NY.

Figure 78. *The Vase of Urine Held by a Dead Doctor.* Buffalmacco, detail from *Trionfo della Morte* (Triumph of Death; fig. 77 above), fresco, c. 1343. Pisa, Camposanto. Scala / Art Resource, NY.

when he was in contemplation, recognized that a doctor with a vair [who appeared to him] was really a devil." The fresco shows a well-dressed individual on horseback, as his profession requires, at the top of a little bridge: he is a doctor but a false one, betrayed by the claws that poke out from under the hem of his dress. He is turning around toward Macarius (who is holding his book of holy meditations firmly open) while pointing with a sweeping gesture to the monks who are heading into the city, where they will certainly be exposed to temptation. Hanging from the belt of the demon are ampules. Viewers who had read the *Vite dei Santi Padri* (Lives of the Holy Fathers) rendered into the vulgar tongue by the Dominican Domenico Cavalca would have known that in reply to Macarius's query as to why he was carrying so many "vessels," the devil had said, "I am bringing them diverse beverages, so that whoever does not like one will take another, and I will give each of them something to drink."[95]

It is easy to see why doctors were an easy and frequent target for the irony of the novella writers. Boccaccio must have had a very low opinion of the profession, holding its members to be boastful knaves. A certain Maestro Simone is the butt of a practical joke laboriously contrived by two astute painters, Bruno and Buffalmacco (the same Buffalmacco who painted the Pisan frescoes we were looking at a moment ago). Boccaccio's narrator launches the tale of Maestro Simone, who had studied at the University of Bologna, with a mordant categorical opinion no doubt shared by Boccaccio himself: "We have occasion to see every day how our fellow citizens return to us from Bologna, some as judges, some as doctors, and others as notaries, all decked out in long, flowing robes of scarlet and vair[96] and a good deal of other pompous paraphernalia, and every day we see the results of all this. Among such men was a Master Simone da Villa, richer in family inheritances than in learning, who not long ago returned to Florence, dressed in scarlet robes and wearing a doctor's hood—a doctor of medicine, according to what he called himself."[97]

Bruno, in order to establish a friendship with Doctor Simone, "painted a Lenten mural in his dining room, a Lamb of God over the entrance to his bedroom, and a urinal [urine container] over the front door to his shop, so that people who needed his help could tell his house from the others; and in one of his loggias he painted for him the battle between the mice and the cats, which, according to the doctor, was too beautiful for words."[98] The derisive significance of the objects Bruno chose to paint is obvious: the urine container, which was indeed the principal diagnostic instrument of doctors, is here highlighted as though it were the only one—whereas Simone himself points out that "as you have been able to observe, I possess the loveliest books and the most elegant wardrobe of any doctor in Florence . . . I wear gloves and long robes. . . ."[99] The Agnus Dei was frequently depicted on amulets for small children and pregnant women,[100] which is as much as to say, doctors and medicine are of very little use. The "picture symbolizing Lent," if it followed the

Figure 79. *Lent*. Pieter Brueghel the Elder, detail from *The Battle between Carnival and Lent*, oil on panel, 1559. Vienna Kunsthistorisches Museum.

description found in the popular *Contrasto* (Comparison) between Lent and Carnival,[101] will have shown Lent as a woman made gaunt and ugly by fasting and penance, not an auspicious subject for a doctor, who is supposed to make you feel healthy and look good. In this connection, one can't help thinking of the famous *Battle between Carnival and Lent* of Pieter Brueghel the Elder, though it is of course much later (1559), in which the undernourished and pallid figure of Lent rolls along on a trolley brandishing a paddle with a couple of herrings (fig. 79)[102]: a comic figure meant to arouse laughter, in strident contrast to the gravity in which Maestro Simone wraps himself.

The "battle of the mice and the cats" requires a little more detailed analysis. We can start with an allusion in the Latin fabulist Phaedrus to a battle between weasels and mice: "Defeated and put to flight by the weasels (their story is *painted* even on the walls of low taverns), the mice gathered trembling round their narrow holes, and by squeezing in, escaped death." The reference by Phaedrus to low taverns indicates the social status of the intended audience.[103] The *Esopo toscano* (Tuscan Aesop) of the fourteenth century also includes a fable about a weasel, mice, and a peasant, the last two derisively portrayed: "Madame weasel meanwhile happened to visit the peasant's house, and there she found that *her special enemies,* the mice, had settled in there, so she *laid siege to them* and in a short while had killed and eaten them all."[104] But the domestic cat was gradually taking the place of the weasel as the primary foe of mice, and in the *Katomyomachia,* a short twelfth-century poem in Greek by the poet Theodorus Prodromus (1100–1156 or 1170), a feline battles against the mice for the first time.[105] This subject appears in a handful of miniatures and in one large and spectacular fresco from about 1150 (fig. 80) in the chapel of Saint John at Pürgg in Styria (Austria).[106] Here the mice, armed with bows and arrows and ensconced in a city with crenelated walls and towers, are defending themselves against the assault of the cats, who under the shelter of their shields and with swords on their belts, seem to be gaining the upper hand. For my part, I note a bas-relief of the thirteenth

Figure 80. *The Battle of the Mice and the Cats.* Fresco, c. 1150. Pürgg, nave of the Chapel of Saint John (Styria, Austria).

Figure 81. *The Battle of the Mice and the Cats.* Bas-relief, thirteenth century. Tarragona, Spain, cathedral cloister.

Figure 82. *The Great Battle of the Mice and the Cats.* Woodcut, in -4°, no place, no publisher, November 1521. From F. V. Essling, *Livres à figures vénitiennes,* 2 vols. (Paris: Olschki-H. Leclerc, 1909), vol. 2, p. 421, no. 2111.

century, crowning the capital of a column in the cloister of the Cathedral of Tarragona (fig. 81),[107] in which we see the cats sinking their teeth into the mice and the funeral of a cat, a feline gravedigger standing ready with his hoe to dig a grave. Boccaccio alludes to the story of the battle on the assumption that his readers know it already, and it continued to circulate. We can read it in a short sixteenth-century poem by an anonymous author, one very close to Teofilo Folengo (or perhaps even Folengo himself), "La gran battaglia de li gatti e de li sorzi. Cosa nuova bellissima da ridere e da piacere" (The great battle of the cats and the mice. Something new and very fine, for laughter and pleasure), which circulated in a large number of printed editions, accompanied by a woodcut print (fig. 82).[108] Through exactly which strands of transmission Boccaccio knew the theme of the battle of the mice and the cats I cannot say; but I may observe that the large cat wearing a shield strapped to its back in the fresco at Pürgg is a motif found in the woodcuts as well[109] and that the funeral of the cat represented at Tarragona is narrated with emphasis in both the *Katomyomachia* and in the Folenghian text (strophes 36–38). Hence it seems to me probable that the battle of the mice and the cats to which Boccaccio refers was a narrative very close to the Folenghian one because a series of passages in the latter, as we shall see below, match the character and the profession of the boastful Simone very closely, as do several of the turns in the plot of the novella. Analogous passages, known to Boccaccio's readers, must have heightened the comic effect of the dialogues between the two painters and Maestro Simone, the foolish and presumptuous master of the house.

The two painters make Simone believe that they belong to a group that "goes on expeditions" at night, meaning that through magic arts its members enjoy splendid banquets and the company of the most beautiful women, whose chambers, with their marvelous beds, Bruno describes as "like being in Paradise, and they are as fragrant as the spice jars in your shop when you're pounding your cumin."[110] "And just how these lady weavers work their treadles and pull your loom reeds for you nice and tight right up to themselves to produce a fine close fabric I leave to your own imagination!"[111] the painter concludes, elaborating a salacious metaphor based on the work done by women at the loom (fig. 83). These miraculous accounts titillate the credulous fool more and more, occasioning another reflection from Boccaccio's narrator: "The doctor, whose knowledge probably did not extend any further than the treatment of milk rashes in suckling children, took Bruno's remarks to be the gospel truth." He lets himself be convinced that he is beloved of, and awaited by, the "countess of Civillari, who was the most beautiful thing to be found in the entire *culattario* [the whole range of rumps or bottoms] of the human race."[112] Civillari, explained a commentator on Boccaccio, Francesco Alunno,[113] "is an alleyway of that name in Florence, above the monastery of San Jacopo a Ripoli, a place in which people defecate quite freely. There certain holes or ditches are dug as receptacles for sewage, and then when the time comes laborers use the excrement to fertilize the gardens."[114] This malodorous place accounts for all the details of the subsequent description of the countess of Civillari: "She is a very great lady, for there are few homes in the world in which she does not have some jurisdiction . . . whenever she is in the vicinity, she makes her presence smelled, even though she usually stays aloof; but it was not long ago that she passed by your door one night on her way to the Arno to wash her feet and to take a breath of fresh air; but her usual residence is in the town of Laterina."[115] This is the name of a real town in the Valdarno, but it sounds so much like

Figure 83. *A Woman Weaving on a Horizontal Loom with Treadles.* Miniature, 1421. Milan, Biblioteca Ambrosiana, MS G 301, fol. 3r (from the Umiliati).

latrina (latrine) that it automatically creates a pun. The sergeants of Madonna Civillari "carry the rod and the bucket," the working tools of those whose job it was to empty ordure from lavatories, and their individual names are all heavily suggestive. Bruno can refer one moment to the sweet aromas in a drug and spice shop, and the next to the fetor and filth of a barnyard: in the medieval streets it could easily happen that as you turned a corner the fragrant smell of bread in the oven was effaced by the violent stench of leather being tanned or meat turning bad in a butcher's. It was equally normal to come upon men relieving themselves freely, along the river at night or in places a bit isolated but still in the city, like Civillari, the alleyway near the monastery of San Jacopo a Ripoli.[116]

By now we begin to see what the two practical jokers are planning; naturally they make a show of reluctance before revealing the big secret, apparently letting themselves be convinced by the proofs of courage Simone gives them: he once beat a poor, skinny prostitute, and he braves the cold of nighttime with "only" a fur for covering. These actually show what a pusillanimous and abject character he is.[117] Finally the big night arrives. The doctor, following the instructions of Bruno and Buffalmacco, is supposed to leave the house in secret, dressed in his best suit, "the scarlet robe in which I received my doctorate," and go to Santa Maria Novella, where he is supposed to climb up "onto one of those raised tombs, the ones just recently constructed outside Santa Maria Novella," and there await the arrival of "a black horned creature," on which he is to seat himself, but only if he feels no fear and does not invoke God and the saints.[118] The doctor promises, gets dressed, and goes at night to the appointed place, where he waits a long time on the freezing marble of the tomb, trembling with cold and fear. Buffalmacco, "who was tall and husky, managed to get one of those masks which were worn during certain celebrations that are no longer held today [a piece of precious information about medieval amusements and group festivities], and putting on a black fur coat inside out,[119] he disguised himself to look like a bear, except for his mask, which had a devil's face and sported horns."[120] Everything turns out the way the two friends had planned. The cowardly Simone is gripped with panic when he sees this unusual mount approaching and immediately asks for the grace of God; the "beast" carries him, quite roughly, to Civillari, where he is hurled into the ditch. With much effort, "totally besmirched from head to toe, sorrowful and wretched," he scrambles out, minus his headgear, and returns home to receive the furious reprimand of his wife, who suspects him of wanting to betray her. Finally, he is loudly reproached again the next day by the two painters, who in the meantime have drawn and painted bruises and scratches all over their own bodies and who make Simone believe that those marks are the consequence of punishment inflicted on themselves because he, Simone, had not done as he had promised. Seeking their pardon, therefore, he showers them afresh with invitations and other favors, so that the jest goes on and on.

Let us now return for a moment to the subjects of the frescoes painted by Bruno to denote the qualifications of Simone: a container of urine and the battle of the mice and the cats. The short Folenghian poem "La gran battaglia de li gatti e de li sorzi" begins like this:

> In the time when the animals talked[121]
> and more liberty was granted them
> before envy and its diverse ills
> came to disturb all their peace
> there reigned a king of gotti (glasses) and urine containers
> of gatti (cats), I mean; who with noble countenance
> had been in battle with a thousand thrushes
> and was the emperor of Gattaglia (all the cats)
> The name he went by was Gattone
>
> --
>
> Gattone, excrementific and potent, had
> ten kingdoms under his crown
> each of these kings so powerful in arms
> that he would have fled from anyone
> and would not have faced up to anything at all;
> throughout the world resounded the fame
> of this magnanimous lord and his kings
> for wreaking havoc on sardines and shrimp.[122]

The ten kings share with their emperor self-conceit, cowardice, the propensity to defraud—all character traits of Maestro Simone; they protect themselves with urine containers (the fourth king had "a clean urine container for a helmet") and are clad in armor made of excrement, a detail that matches very closely the climax of the adventure of Simone and the "countess of Civillari."[123] The description in the poem of the cats outfitted for war is a parody of the instruments used by doctors, their typical outfit, and the hollowness of their learning. The cats ride *ingistare* and *mortari*; the former are glass carafes with wide bottoms and long thin necks used for inspecting urine (in a moment we will see one being used by another of Boccaccio's doctors, Mazzeo della Montagna); the latter are mortars in which medicinal ingredients are ground. They wear "helmets of fur and outer garments made of squirrel backs, and vair," and they grip "lances of fog and smoke and wind, and of a 'leave me alone' full of boldness"[124] (that is, full of conceit and cowardice).

Let us now pass to Mazzeo della Montagna from Salerno, "most eminent in surgery," of advanced age and with a young and beautiful wife: a man obviously destined to be cuckolded. The doctor, in a case presented to him, does not risk his reputation: the situation is desperate, and Mazzeo succeeds in convincing the relatives that he is about to operate on a man who is practically dead already.

> It happened that a sick patient with a festering leg was placed under the surgeon's care: after the doctor had examined his diseased leg, he told the man's relatives that unless a gangrenous bone in the leg was removed, it would be necessary to amputate the entire limb, or he would die, and since there was no way of guaranteeing them that with the removal of the bone the patient would be cured, he advised them that he would not take the case unless they were willing to consider the man as already a lost cause; his relatives, having agreed to these conditions, then placed him in the surgeon's care. The doctor realized that the patient would not bear the pain of the operation or even allow himself to be treated without first being drugged,[125] and since he had to wait until evening to perform this operation, that morning he had a liquid distilled from one of his special prescriptions which, when drunk, would make a person sleep for as long as the doctor thought was necessary to operate on him; and he had this liquid sent to his home, and there he put it in his bedroom without mentioning what it was to anyone. When the hour of vespers arrived, and the surgeon was about to go to his patient, some very good friends of his in Amalfi sent word that he should drop everything he was doing and go there at once because there had just been a violent brawl in which many people had been wounded. Postponing until the following morning the operation on the leg, the surgeon took a boat and sailed to Amalfi.[126]

Mazzeo's wife's lover immediately took advantage of this absence; but as the man entered the bedroom, he saw the *guastadetta* (little carafe) containing the distillate of

Figure 84. *Two Niches in a Wall.*
Taddeo Gaddi, detail from *Stories
from the Life of the Virgin,* fresco,
first half of the fourteenth
century. Florence, Santa Croce,
Cappella Baroncelli.

opium "on the windowsill," and thinking it was water, he drank it and fell into a
deep sleep.

The mistake happened because this was a room without any cupboards, like all
medieval rooms, which were provided at most with a few open shelves in niches (fig
84). The opium-based anesthetic was therefore simply left sitting out in the open.
Equally casual was the scheduling of the operation, which was at the mercy of
events. Having abandoned his poor patient with a leg full of gangrene, what assistance was Mazzeo, alone in his boat, going to be able to offer to a crowd of wounded
waiting for him at the dock in Amalfi? Boccaccio's irony is evident; and beyond that
we are struck by the hazardousness and the violence of everyday life.

Meanwhile, Mazzeo's wife was of course eager to take advantage of his absence as
well. But instead she found her lover so deep in sleep that she thought he was dead.
To avoid scandal she followed the advice of an alert servant who the day before had
noticed a coffin left in the street in front of a carpenter's shop, evidently for lack of
space in the work area. So the lover was placed in the coffin at night and left in front
of the carpenter's shop. We can follow the rest of the story in Boccaccio's own

words, for he places a summary at the head of each novella: "The chest is carried off
with the man inside by two usurers to their home; when the lover comes to his
senses he is arrested as a thief; the lady's servant tells the authorities that she was the
one who put him inside the chest stolen by the usurers, whereupon the lover escapes
the gallows and the moneylenders are condemned to pay a fine for making off with
the chest."[127]

WITH THE HELP OF GOD

Maestro Simone and Mazzeo della Montagna, the former trained at the prestigious
University of Bologna, the latter a graduate of the celebrated medical school at
Salerno, do not give brilliant displays of professionalism. The statutes of Città di
Castello specify that the city's doctor is required to "be expert, qualified, and experienced in the art of medicine," so that *with the help of God* he will be able to cure the
diseases of the body and preserve health,"[128] and probably the words in italics were
not just a meaningless formula.

Divine intervention was indispensable all too often; yet before turning to God,
people preferred to direct their prayers to saints who would intercede for them,
saints who had no hesitation in leaving their heavenly abode and swooping down to
earth—Santa Chiara, for example, summoned by the wailing of a mother whose
child had been seized and partly devoured by a wolf (fig. 85). The saints also understood, and granted, more humble requests, ones commensurate to the modest lives
of those who invoked them—like Santa Bona,[129] who came to cure a horse that
unexpectedly fell and lay stretched out on the floor of the stable: "It was lying

Figure 85. *Santa Chiara Comes to
the Aid of a Child Bitten by a Wolf.*
Giovanni di Paolo, part of
the predella of the dispersed
Pala di Santa Chiara, tempera
panel, middle of the fifteenth
century. Houston, Museum
of Fine Arts.

Figure 86. *The Healing of Juan
of Lérida.* From the cycle of
the *Life of Saint Francis,* fresco,
beginning of the fourteenth
century. Assisi, Basilica
Superiore. Scala / Art Resource, NY.

motionless, and did not move even if it was tugged by the feet, or by the ears, or by the tail." The whole family kept watch in consternation. At a certain point the wife of the owner threw herself on her knees, pleading with the saint to consent to save the animal "in view of the seriousness of the loss." The horse immediately "ignoring all the others who went on continually touching it, turned its gaze on the woman and held it fixed on her alone, as though acquiescing that Bona's help should be summoned." And an instant later the saint, responding to the heartfelt and intense look on the animal's face, mirroring that of her human devotees, made the animal jump to its feet.[130]

At times the saints carried down with them from heaven the medicaments that were needed, as San Francesco did when he came to cure Juan of Lérida, who was gravely wounded. The story is told in the fresco of the Basilica Superiore at Assisi (fig. 86). The wife of the wounded man, followed by her servant, leaves his bedside—

unable to bear the stench of the wounds, the biography of Francesco by Bonaventura informs us—after she has heard the prognosis of the doctor, who opens his hands in a gesture of hopelessness. Yet beside the bed stands San Francesco, who has come down from paradise in the company of two angels, one of whom has in his hand a small container with the celestial medicine, so much more efficacious than the useless balms of humans. The two heavenly creatures, who do not feature in the biography, are an effective visual allusion to the new abode of the saint. The healing of Juan of Lérida is a miracle that rewards devotion and at the same time confirms and propagates the fame of the saint and his power to heal. In fact, the undertitle[131] explained: "The doctors gave up hope for Juan of Lérida, who was mortally wounded. The blessed Francesco healed him on the instant, undoing the bandages with his sacred

✦ Figure 87. *A Pharmacy.* Fresco, 1488–1495. Castle of Issogne, Val d'Aosta. Scala / Art Resource, NY.

hands and touching the wounds with the greatest gentleness; Juan, at the time he
was wounded, had invoked Francesco with great devotion."[132]

PHARMACIES AND EX-VOTOS

The pharmacists and spice dealers were also well aware of the limitations of their
own remedies. (Doctors, pharmacists, and spice dealers constituted a single amor-
phous professional category, since spices and spice mixtures were prescribed and
sold as medicines as well as for use in cooking and also in cloth dyeing.) In one of
the frescoes that decorate the castle of Issogne in Val d'Aosta, painted between 1488
and 1495, many details of the shop of a pharmacist/spice dealer are shown (fig. 87).
A woman is purchasing medicinal herbs, which the pharmacist is weighing out for
her on a balance; further to the left an older partner is keeping the books; at the
right, a shop assistant of low social level, with his clothing in tatters, is carrying out
the long and tiring job of crushing the various substances with a heavy bronze pes-
tle inside a bronze mortar. Behind the counter are arrayed, in a carefully ordered
row, all the possible remedies, beginning with the ones for sale in a row of vases, the
contents of each made clear by a label in Latin.[133] Yet these preparations must not
invariably have been efficacious, if the pharmacy itself—as in this painting—also
retailed ex-votos of wax.[134] Here, reading from left to right, we see the following
hanging: a leg up to knee height, a hand, a foot, a grateful child with hands joined,
and a little horse.

In vain Franco Sacchetti railed against the practice of ex-votos: "These vows, and
others like them, are made every day, and they smack more of idolatry than Christian faith. And I, the writer, once saw an individual who had lost a cat make a vow
that if he found it again, he would offer a wax model of it to Our Lady of Orto San
Michele; and so he did. Oh, isn't this not just lack of faith, but a mockery of God
and Our Lady and all his Saints? He wants our heart and our mind, and does not go
asking for waxen images or for this sort of conceit and vanity."[135] Even animals
sometimes have the ability to take the place of humans, invoking and receiving
salvation, an event properly regarded as miraculous (fig. 88). We are in Portugal, at
Terena. A poor mule was lying in the stable with its hind legs paralyzed and swollen,
until one day its owner decided to have it put down, since it was no longer any use
for work. On the way to its death, the mule, which was dragging itself along, suddenly recovered when it got to the door of the Church of Santa Maria. Shortly after,
it actually came into the church and went down on its knees, humble and grateful,
before a statue of the Madonna and Child. The faithful then made haste to bring
piles of candles "on behalf of the mule," so to speak, in happy thansgiving.[136]

It was a very reassuring thing, the thought that one could entrust oneself to the
invisible, but efficacious, protection of a saint, who would always watch over his or

Como un ome bõ tĩia un seu muu doẽte τ mãdo desfollar a seu cõ taio.

Como o mãcebo se posou a almorzar τ o muu fugiu pela porta.

Como o muu se foi pa a ygreia de sãta mª fico chegou apar dela foy são.

Co o mãcebo achou o muu são τ chamou a gẽte q̃ uisse a mauilla.

Co o muu entrou na ygreia de sãta mª τ ficou os gẽollos ãto altar.

Co toda a gẽte loaron muyt a santa maria por este miragre.

her devotees. Even in cases in which it was perfectly evident that human intervention had resolved the problem, the merit of the positive relief was always attributed to the saint. Let us take one of the miracles of Saint Louis as an example (fig. 89). A three-year-old babe named Marote had gone to play with her older brother along the bank of a stream, but the brother had no wish to bother with his little sister, and Marote instead began to dip in water with a small pitcher until she lost her balance and fell into the stream. The screams of her nurse drew a number of men, who pulled her out. In the miniature the nurse orders that the babe be tied to a tree head down in order to drain out the water she has swallowed; then the same woman immerses the little one in a hot bath, and puts her to bed, well covered and warmed by the crackling fire in the hearth. Apparently nothing worked. From our point of view it is perfectly clear that the nurse's actions to save the baby girl were already taking effect; but the nurse herself believed that she had to go further and pray to Saint Louis, who naturally intervened and brought little Marote back to life. The grateful

Figure 88. *The Miraculous Recovery of the Mule.* Miniature, 1281–1284, from Alfonso X the Wise, *Cantigas de Santa María.* Florence, Biblioteca Nazionale Centrale, MS B. R. 20, fol. 112r.

Figure 89. *Saint Louis Saves Little Marote from Death by Drowning.* Miniature, end of the fifteenth century, from *Vie et miracle de Saint Louis.* Paris, Bibliothèque Nationale, MS Fr. 2829, fol. 98v.

woman, in the conclusion of this painted narrative, made a visit with the baby to the church at Saint-Denis, where the tomb of the saint-king lay.

WOMEN'S CURES

The initiative and the actions taken to save Marote all came from the nurse and not from the men who ran to help. Her reactions are natural enough, when we remember that women, confined to the house and grappling with the problems of raising offspring and looking after the family, had a "functional" incentive to know about remedies and potions. Their wisdom, often jealously transmitted from mother to daughter, extended to plants and their properties. Proof of this was the unhappy Ghismunda, daughter of Tancredi, the protagonist of a novella of Boccaccio, who knows the powers of herbs and manipulates them herself with tragic expertise.

> Tancredi was sometimes in the habit of visiting his daughter's bedroom to spend a little time talking to her, and then he would leave. One day after eating, while the lady (whose name was Ghismunda) was in the garden with all her attendants, he went there without being observed or heard by anyone and entered her bedroom. Finding the windows closed and the bed curtains drawn back, and not wishing to take her away from her amusement, Tancredi sat down on a small divan [carello] at the foot of the bed; he leaned his head back on the bed and drew the bed curtain around him—almost as if he were trying to hide himself on purpose—and there he fell asleep.[137]

The missed rendezvous, which then develops into a contretemps with tragic consequences, gives us a chance to note a couple of practices: the utilization of the bedroom during the daytime as a place to receive visits and converse, and the capacity to have extra guests sleep over offered by the "carello" (translated "divan" above), a low chest with cushions and wheels that was kept under the bed and trundled out for use as a seat or a supplementary bed.

The father awakened without signaling his presence when his daughter and her lover entered and got into bed. Only later did he confront Ghismunda, who foresaw that he would take vengeance, and "had poisonous herbs and roots brought to her . . . and she distilled and reduced them to a liquid, in order to have it available if what she feared actually did occur."[138] Her foreboding came true, for her father sent her the heart of her lover in a cup. Ghismunda covered it with her tears, poured out the poison, drank it, and awaited her death with composure.

In another novella by Boccaccio, a woman, in this case the mother of Gentile Carisendi, once again shows herself able to cope with an emergency. Her son, having brought home a lady, Madonna Catalina, who had been buried because she was believed to be dead but was in fact still faintly drawing breath, "his mother, a wise and worthy woman . . . skilfully brought the lady back to her senses by means of hot baths and the warmth of the fire."[139]

It is always, and only, women, who step in and provide services of a kind we would call "medical" for a host of female illnesses, who assist at childbirth, who take care of giving the newborn child its first bath, and who are capable, if necessary, of preparing the right medicines. This familiarity with the handling of recipes and ingredients could be very dangerous for them: far more women than men were identified as witches in the Middle Ages. In the persecution of these unfortunates, almost all of whom were condemned to be burned to death, the resentment and prejudice of learned, male medicine toward female folk medicine, not to speak of professional rivalry, played a part. A miniature from the beginning of the fifteenth century shows this clearly; it is taken from the *Épistre d'Othéa* of Christine de Pizan (c. 1364–1431), in which Aesculapius, the god of medicine, is contrasted to the sorceress Circe, who enchanted the companions of Ulysses and enslaved them with her beauty. Aesculapius is incarnated in the form of a doctor of the fifteenth century, inspecting urine, while Circe—despite her legendary powers of seduction—is an old crone who is piercing toads for her poisonous concoctions. On one side we have a man and official medicine; on the other, a woman guilty of being aged, and empirical medicine bordering on spells and sorcery.[140] Witches were accused of preparing magic unguents and using supernatural means to cause harm, especially to small babies. In fact, the rate of puerperal and infantile mortality was so high that we can understand how, in ignorance of the real causes, it was all too easy to hold responsible the persons who had had most to do with the newborn, with the mother, or with the care of small children.

Sometimes, though, the scapegoat became the devil himself, who was accused of having snatched the newborn babe and placed a little devil in the cradle instead: such a case is narrated, for example, in the legend of Santo Stefano (fig. 90). Mothers might become convinced that babies who were low in body weight and often sick were "changelings" of this kind; if the baby failed to grow, that was the surest sign of all that the devil had made a switch, for a "changeling" never alters. In the hope of forcing the devil to bring back the stolen baby, the "changeling" was subjected to cruel rituals and often abandoned and left to die.[141]

Medieval men and women moved in a natural world whose laws in large measure evaded them, and perceived phenomena the causes of which (microbes, for example) were unknown, while on the other hand they were conditioned, to an extremely high degree, by religion, the frame of reference for every human action. When angels, demons, and saints are ever present and prompt either to help or to hurt, the line between faith and superstition, between a spell and a miracle, is ambiguous.

How often it was a challenge, even for churchmen themselves, to distinguish, with the help of the inscrutable divine will, between the works of Lucifer and those of the angel of light, between the true saint and the impostor, the miracle and the fake. The expectation of the supernatural, the acquaintance with the other world, explain, at least in part, the consensus surrounding the witch hunt; the victims were

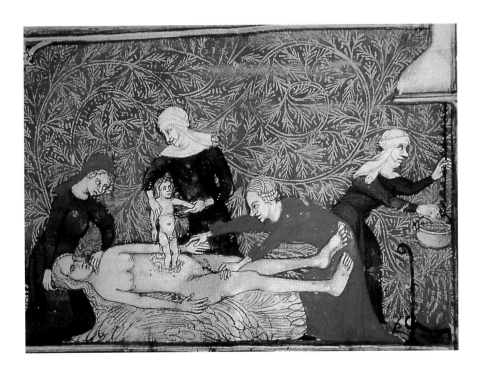

Figure 90. *A Devil Steals the New-born Stefano, a Future Saint, and Puts a Little Devil in His Cradle.* Detail from the *Vita di santo Stefano* (Life of Saint Stephen), tempera panel, beginning of the fifteenth century. Frankfurt am Main, Städel Museum.

Figure 91. *The Birth of Julius Caesar by Caesarean Section.* Miniature, beginning of the fourteenth century, from *Les faits des Romains.* Paris, Bibliothèque Nationale, Nouvelle Acq. Fr., MS 3576, fol. 197.

really believed to be witches, not only by the Inquisition that interrogated, tortured, and judged them but also by those who knew them well as innocuous neighbors, yet who were always prepared to see them suddenly in a different light.

The experience and the ability of women in obstetrics and gynecology were however too valuable for them constantly to be cast in a bad light. It was women who were charged, should the mother die during childbirth, with surgically extracting the baby from her womb by cesarean section. In a fourteenth-century miniature from *Les faits des Romains* (fig. 91), the birth of Julius Caesar[142] is represented, as usual, in a medieval setting. We are in a room in a castle, where the dead woman has been laid out on a thick bed of straw to absorb the blood. A woman is lifting a pot of boiling water from the notched rack above the fireplace, where a blaze is crackling; if the baby lives—as Caesar of course does—he will immediately be washed and baptized.

Madonna Catalina, whom we have already met, was expecting a baby when "she happened to be stricken with a serious illness," so that the doctors concluded that she had died. "Since even her closest relatives stated that they had heard from her own lips that she had not been pregnant long enough for the creature to have been perfectly formed, without giving it a second thought and with much weeping, they buried her just as she was, within a tomb in a church nearby."[143] The women relatives of Catalina, in other words, faced the problem of whether or not to perform a cesarean section to save and baptize the baby: for if the fetus, already formed, were to die inside its mother's body, the little soul would not be able to go to paradise.[144] Mothers who died in childbirth together with an unborn but viable baby were normally buried outside consecrated ground, because they were guilty of carrying inside them an unbaptized person; the same fate was reserved for a baby born dead or who died before being baptized.[145]

Women were able to use surgical instruments on dead bodies for other purposes as well. In the official record of the canonization trial of Chiara da Montefalco (1268–1308), we discover that it was her own sister nuns who undertook the task of performing a careful dissection of her body after death in order to locate the cross and the instruments of Christ's Passion—the *Arma Christi* (arms of Christ) that their abbess had always said, while alive, that she carried locked in her heart.[146]

It is always women, and only women, obviously, who are employed in the nativity scenes of the Virgin Mary, of Christ, and of John the Baptist. In the canonical gospels Mary is left to deliver the baby Jesus alone, a situation promptly remedied in the apocryphal ones, which put two midwives at her side. One of the two, Salome, did not believe in the possibility of a virgin birth, and for this profanity was punished by having her arm paralyzed; though since her subsequent repentance was profound, she was pardoned.

Chapter Four

THE LIVES OF CHILDREN

Nature shows the face of a kind mother to the young of all the other species; only in regard to man does she show herself a wicked stepmother . . . on the day of his birth she throws him forth naked on the naked ground to cry and wail forthwith; no other living thing is born to instant tears. . . . Then this unhappy human being is wrapped, and all its limbs bound, to make it understand that it has been delivered into a prison. Only the eyes and the mouth are left free to play their parts, which are to shed tears and to howl. And all this in the best of cases, when the child is the offspring of a king or an emperor. The poor weeping soul lies there, bound hand and foot and presaging a life of torment, for the sole fault of having been born.[1]

Newborn babies in the Middle Ages were indeed wrapped up very tightly, like little mummies, because it was feared that otherwise their delicate bones would develop badly or become crooked. Yet tender devotion was also lavished on them from the start, as we can tell from the many scenes of childbirth in Bible stories that were represented according to the contemporary reality known to the painters. Let us take a look at *The Birth of the Virgin* by the Saint Elsino Master, now in the National Gallery of London (fig. 92). The elderly Anna lies in bed, overcome by exhaustion and pain. Around her bed the curtains have been drawn, as they had to be in medieval rooms, with their lack of heat and their exposure to currents of cold air. "Why do you make warm mattresses stuffed with wool or feathers? To invite the sleep that you need to be well rested. And why do you make curtains? Because

you fear the wind," explained Giordano da Pisa in a sermon that began with a gloss on the evangelical verse "Happy are those who have not seen and yet believe."[2]

Lying beside the bed is an essential piece of medieval furniture: a long low chest, used as we would use a chest of drawers to hold the outer garments and the underclothing of the members of the household, but also as a seat on which to sit and talk and as a table on which to set pitchers and bowls. A servant is approaching Anna to revive her with the breeze from a rectangular fan and offer her something good to eat (the covered hot dish she is carrying probably contains a chicken). In the foreground three women are busy giving the newborn babe her first bath: one is swirling

Figure 92. *The Birth of the Virgin.* The Saint Elsino Master, compartment of a polyptych with the *Vergine dell'umiltà* (The Virgin of Humility), and *Storie della Vergine e di san t'Elsino* (Stories of the Virgin and of Saint Elsino), tempera panel, fourteenth century. London, National Gallery.

Figure 93. *The Nativity.* Rhenish master, tempera panel, beginning of the fifteenth century. Berlin, Dahlem, Staatliche Museen, Gemäldegalerie.

the water in a low tub, while another approaches with a sort of carafe that we are to imagine full of hot water taken a moment ago from the kettle set over a crackling fire in the next room. Mary is very pretty, with her face nestled against the cheek of the nurse who is holding her.

A Rhenish master from the beginning of the fifteenth century has, in turn, narrated the birth of Jesus employing a group of angels to remedy the discomforts suffered by a poor babe who was born practically in the open air on a cold winter night (fig. 93). The traditional scene of the Holy Family here becomes a dreamscape. The

celestial workmen have clambered up a ladder and onto the roof to repair the holes in the covering of thatch. Mary reclines on a soft bed covered with a brocade, while an angel adjusts the pillow behind her head. To regain her strength the Virgin is holding a brimming bowl and a spoon. Jesus, who is certainly capable of doing things that other babies couldn't, has already got to his feet by himself and is going to bring a bit of joy to the elderly Joseph, who is at his carpenter's workbench, holding out two flowers (the ox, the ass, and the manger or feedbox, displaced from their traditional role, are barely visible). In the foreground at the left, a highly wrought golden fountain gleams, from which two angels have just drawn water: one bears two pails hanging from a staff on his shoulder, the other a pitcher, likewise on his shoulder. On the fireplace close by, resting on a solid tripod, there sits a cauldron full of boiling water, and the fire tongs are ready should it be necessary to stir up the embers. A couple of angels are by the fire, warming up the towels that will shortly be used to dry the little one off, and with a touch of delicate refinement, the tub of hot

Figure 94. *A Peasant Returning Home After Work, and His Family.* Miniature, second quarter of the fourteenth century. Turin, Biblioteca Nazionale, MS E. I.1, fol. 310v.

Figure 95. *Isaac in His Cradle Being Fed Milk Through a Horn.* Miniature, fourteenth century, from the *Bible of Jean de Sy.* Paris, Bibliothèque Nationale, MS Fr. 15397, fol. 32v.

water that awaits him is covered with a canopy of embroidered sheeting, so that while he is in the bath the baby will be enveloped in warm vapor. A blond maid with a little pitcher in her hand stands ready to take care of everything.

It was normal for newborns to be placed in a rocking cradle, but it was typically Italian for them to rock longitudinally, along the axis from head to foot, as we see in this miniature (fig. 94): a wife is helping her husband to change his clothes, one of her three children tugs at her clothing to get her attention, and the newborn, swaddled up to his ears, sleeps beatifically. From poles are hanging a bucket, a pitcher, clothing, and linen, all of them kept at a height to escape the dirt of the pavement and attack by mice. Outside Italy Europeans preferred to rock their babies with a lateral motion, from side to side, as shown in a miniature from the fourteenth century (fig. 95).

Sometimes the cradle might be rigged with rope so that it hung from the ceiling right above the parents' bed and they could reach out and make it swing with one arm—an ingenious way to save the space that was at such a premium in cramped medieval houses, but not without its risks, since the ropes might break. A nurse sitting on a bed with her feet resting on a red chest beside it (fig. 96) has maybe pushed a little too hard on one of these swinging cradles, causing a rope to break. The baby has gone flying right out the window and now lies unconscious on the adjacent terrace. But the blessed Agostino Novello is gliding down from heaven to

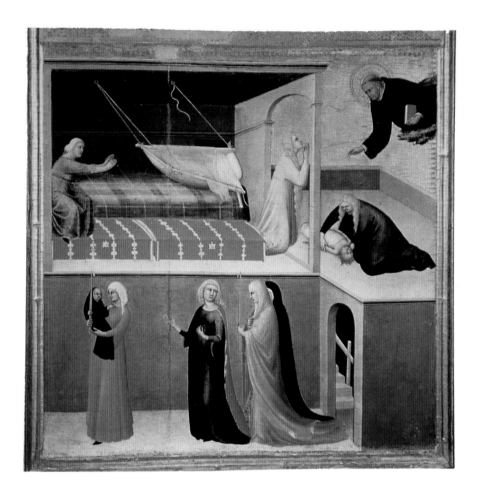

Figure 96. *The Blessed Agostino Novello Saves a Baby Who Has Fallen from a Swinging Cradle.* Simone Martini, detail from the *Pala del beato Agostino Novello* (Altarpiece of the Blessed Agostino Novello), tempera panel, beginning of fourteenth century. Siena, Pinacoteca Nazionale. Scala/Art Resource, NY.

save him. In the lower plane the revived baby, dressed as a friar and grasping a candle in his fist, is being carried by his mother to give thanks, no doubt at the tomb of the blessed rescuer.

Agostino Novello must have kept a special watch over children (the parents of young ones who were injured certainly thought so) because three of the four miracles painted by Simone Martini on the altar piece dedicated to him are concerned with infants. In one miracle, (fig. 97), Agostino descends from on high to heal a baby bitten on the head by a savage dog, which a woman is trying in vain to drive off with blows from a stick. The buildings all have battlements and are perhaps meant to tell us that we are outside the walls of a city. In another (fig. 98), he succeeds with brilliant timing, exceptional even for one of the beatified, in seizing a falling plank that is about to fall on the head of a baby who is already in trouble because he has fallen from a height. The plank came loose and fell off an enclosed balcony, leaving a gap through which we can see the bench the baby had climbed up on to get a better view. This portion of the altar piece is justly famous for the view it offers of narrow twisting medieval streets: so narrow that a knight who was "haughty and discourteous, when he went through the city, especially on horseback, spread his legs so wide that he took up the whole street at the places where it narrowed, so that anyone passing by wound up involuntarily wiping the tips of his shoes for him."[3] The external staircases of the houses (fig. 99) served to clutter and crowd the streets even more, making them discreet and convenient at night for those with criminal intent, opportune places for muggings, thefts, and homicides.[4] At Siena, near the street where the *Umiliati* resided, the houses were so low and the streets so cramped that the friars, when they passed through in a funeral procession, were obliged to lower the processional cross, and completely blocked anyone else from getting through.[5] In Simone Martini's altarpiece the wooden struts that bear the load of balconies and verandas made of wood or masonry encroach on the street (fig. 98) in a desperate attempt to enlarge the small rooms of the houses—unfortunately ensuring that if a fire got started the flames would easily be able to spread. At Siena in 1309 the order was given to tear down a series of protruding galleries, "since the street in which the said galleries are located is too dark and is a fire hazard."[6] As well the overhanging upper stories of the houses created a serious obstacle for those who had to transport bulky loads. The windows were usually unglazed, being covered by wooden shutters that provided shelter from the weather at the cost of plunging the rooms, which were poorly lit to start with, into deep gloom.[7] To prevent clouds of flies from getting in, our friend the elderly Parisian husband advised "keeping the windows tightly closed with waxed canvas, or parchment"[8]; clearly for a bourgeois of the late fourteenth century, even a rich one, glazed windows were still a luxury that was out of reach (fig. 100).

The child saved by a miracle in Simone Martini's altar piece (fig. 98 above), whom we see both tumbling from the balcony and getting up unhurt after his fall, is wearing a long garment with two bands of color; others would have been added to lengthen the garment as he grew.

The cradle went along with the baby when the family was going somewhere: this mother (fig. 101) has hoisted it onto her head, and has two other small children following her, one of whom is holding a spoon and a little pitcher for use as a nursing bottle. Two more little ones, not yet able to walk, have been placed in a sort of pannier that their father has slung over his shoulder. Five children in a row—but

Figure 97. *The Blessed Agostino Novello Saves a Baby Bitten in the Head by a Savage Dog.* Simone Martini, detail from the *Pala del beato Agostino Novello* (Altarpiece of the Blessed Agostino Novello), tempera panel, beginning of fourteenth century. Siena, Pinacoteca Nazionale. Scala / Art Resource, NY.

Figure 98. *The Blessed Agostino Novello Saves a Baby Who Is Falling from a Balcony.* Simone Martini, detail from the *Pala del beato Agostino Novello* (Altarpiece of the Blessed Agostino Novello), tempera panel, beginning of fourteenth century. Siena, Pinacoteca Nazionale. Scala / Art Resource, NY.

Figure 99. *A Scene from the Love Story of Gianni da Procida and Restituta di Marin Bolghero*. Miniature, fifteenth century, from Boccaccio, *Decameron*, 5.6. Paris, Bibliothèque de l'Arsenal, MS 5070, fol. 201r. External stairs are depicted.

Figure 100. *The Tryst Interuppted*. Miniature, fifteenth century, from Boccaccio, *Decameron*, 5.10. Paris, Bibliothèque de l'Arsenal, MS 5070, fol. 215v. The miniature shows a house of extremely wealthy people: the staircase is internal and the windows are glazed with colored glass.

how many would survive? It has been calculated that in the Middle Ages one baby in three died before the age of five.⁹ The causes were varied; many babies, the majority of them apparently girls, died of suffocation in their parents' beds, since their mothers preferred to have them there at night to make it easier to nurse them without having to get up (fig. 102): simple carelessness? or infanticide, either passive or truly premeditated?¹⁰ Overlarge families might not be able to bear the burden of so many births, and girls were even less welcome than boys, since the cost of marrying them off was a drag on the household economy. Once they were married, daughters would leave their family of origin and would no longer be there to help their aging parents. Scholars are not entirely agreed on how to interpret these deaths, but in any case they were so frequent that they form a separate category in the confessors' manuals. The canonist Burchard of Worms (c. 965–1025) prescribes forty straight days of bread and water in cases in which there was doubt about the cause of death, or in

Figure 101. *A Family in Flight.* Miniature, end of the thirteenth century, from the *Apocalypse en image.* Paris, Bibliothèque Nationale, MS Fr. 13096, fol. 60v.

Figure 102. *Santa Francesca Romana Revives a Baby Smothered in Its Mother's Bed.* Antoniazzo Romano, detail from a cycle dedicated to this saint, fresco, 1468. Rome, Monastero delle Oblate di S. Francesca Romana (Tor de' Specchi).

which it was not clear on whom to lay the blame, the mother or the father; but three years of fasting on bread and water, on the prescribed days, if the cause of death was ascertained to be parental negligence.[11]

A baby could die because its mother did not have enough milk to nourish it; Saint Catherine told her confessor that her mother had been forced to choose between giving milk to her, or to her twin: the twin was sent to a wet nurse, and died.[12] The custom of sending an infant to a hired wet nurse in the country was widespread in the Middle Ages, in all social classes, even though it often turned out to be fatal for the newborn child—in Italy, seventeen percent of the time.[13] Many little ones were not strong enough to make the trip, or died when they got there because of the low quality of the milk, which was either not nutritious or else was provided too seldom. On the other hand, it was believed that milk from a pregnant woman was harmful to a baby, and since a fertile woman gave birth on average every eighteen months,[14] the help of a wet nurse was required if family size was to increase.

The baby grows, and finally leaves the cradle; a baby walker will be there to help him take his first steps. At this stage the child is protected by a long garment that comes down to the ankles and that buttons at the front, the same for both sexes, and by amulets of different kinds, most often a small branch of coral.[15] No underclothing is worn.[16] Naturally it is through images of the Madonna and Baby Jesus that we can catch a glimpse of medieval childhood; in this delicious Flemish miniature of c. 1440 (fig. 103), the Child is trotting inside a baby walker and is saying to this mother, who is intent on weaving a trim of different colors, "I am your consolation" (*Ego sum solacium tuum*).[17]

What did children play at once they were old enough to walk and run? Some diversions were restricted to wintertime: in December, when the pigs were slaughtered, the children would blow pig bladders up like balloons (fig. 104), and when it snowed, they went into the streets to throw snowballs (fig. 105). Let us listen to the memories of Jean Froissart, a French historian (1337–after 1404): "I wanted to be the best at catching butterflies. When I succeeded in capturing them I tied a light thread to them and then I let them fly again. I played at 'catch the wolf's tail.' Often I used a stick to make a play horse, which I called Grisette (fig. 106). From morning to evening I played with a top and a string that I used to spin it (fig. 107),[18] and I

Figure 103. *The Holy Family.* Miniature, c. 1440, from the *Book of Hours of Catherine de Clèves.* New York, Pierpont Morgan Library, MS 917.

Figure 104. *A Child Makes a Balloon of a Pig Bladder.* Miniature, fifteenth century, from the *Breviarium* of Ercole d'Este. Modena, Biblioteca Estense, MS V.G.11 (= lat. 424, fol. 6v).

Figure 105. *Adults and Children Playing in the Snow.* Miniature, fifteenth century, from the *Heures de la duchesse de Bourgogne.* Chantilly, Musée Condé, MS 76, fol. 12. Réunion de Musées Nationaux / Art Resource, NY.

Figure 106. *A Child Using a Broomstick for a Horse.* Detail from *The Ages of Man.* Miniature, fifteenth century, from Bartholomeus Anglicus, *On the properties of things (Liber De proprietatibus rerum).* Paris, Bibliothèque Nationale, MS Fr. 218, fol. 95.

Figure 107. *The Baby Jesus with His Top beside Him.* Meister Bertram, detail from the Buxtehuder Altar, tempera panel, c. 1400. Hamburg, Kunsthalle.

often used to blow water through a reed."[19] Water fights must have been a very popular form of recreation, if they could be used by a mystic as a simile to explain the effects of a figure that came to life: Giacomo Bianconi, finding himself before a crucifix in church one day at Bevagna, near Perugia, suddenly had his face and cloak soaked with blood and water that burst from the wound in the side of Christ "the way boys like to make water spurt through a reed."[20] The obvious reference to the miracle of the cure of Longinus[21] is combined with a happy moment gleaned from daily life.

We know more about medieval children's games ever since a whole collection of toys made of clay was discovered during the nineteenth century in Strasbourg, in the workshop of a thirteenth-century potter: bird-shaped whistles, miniature tiles and pitchers, tiny moneyboxes, little dolls, and diminutive horses with riders on their backs (fig. 108).[22] Children loved to fight battles with wooden swords, compete in

Figure 108. Terra-cotta toys. Thirteenth century. Strasbourg, Musée de l'Oeuvre Notre-Dame.

✤ Figure 109. *The Baby Jesus with His Toy Windmill.* Master of Vivoin, detail from *The Virgin and Saint Benedict,* panel, fifteenth century. Le Mans, Musée de Tessé.

Figure 110. *The Device of the Printer Jean Moulinet.* Drawing, 1500. Paris, Bibliothèque Nationale, Imprimés, Réserve, Ye 1077. A little windmill is mounted in a nut.

play tournaments, play hide-and-seek; games were played with balls, and sometimes even with wooden sticks too, in a remote precursor of modern field hockey. They liked to run and jump, or spin the blades of a miniature windmill inserted in a nut— a toy that was the favorite plaything of the Baby Jesus, according to the painters, since the blades evoked the cross (fig. 109), and that became the emblem of the publishing house of Jean Moulinet (fig. 110; the pun on "little mill" is obvious).[23]

The expected span of a human life was short, and so was the duration of the carefree period of infancy. Children began to work very young: William of Norwich was already helping in the shop of a seller of furs when he was eight years old.[24] We still have a record of contracts made by boys of ten or twelve years to enter apprenticeships in the arts of painting chests and working silk.[25] The boy whose blond head we can just see peeking out from behind the counter of the seller of footwear, painted by Lorenzetti in the *Effects of good government in the city,* is right where he belongs (fig. 34 above).[26] There were worse fates, like being sold as a slave, perhaps to Jews or "Saracens" who engaged in this trade: a problem taken up by the Lateran Council of 1179. The practice was more generalized than that, however, and Christians were involved too: the merchant of Prato, Francesco Datini (1335–1410) wrote to a friend with instructions to purchase a little slave girl.[27] One of Boccaccio's novellas has as its protagonist Teodoro, who was stolen as a child in Armenia and sold by the Genovese in Sicily: "During the time when good King William ruled Sicily [between 1166 and 1189] there was on the island a nobleman called Messer Amerigo Abate da Trapani who, with other worldly goods he possessed, was well furnished with many children. Therefore, he was in need of servants, and when certain galleys arrived from the Levant belonging to Genoese pirates who had captured many young boys during coastal raids in Armenia, believing that these boys were Turkish, he bought some of them. While they all looked like they were of peasant stock, there was one among them whose noble and better appearance seemed to reflect some other origin, and he was called Teodoro."[28]

Our sources also report the frequent kidnapping of children, sometimes in order to obtain a ransom from their relatives, but principally in order to sell them as slaves. The unfortunate parents of stolen children turned for solace to paintings of the miracles of Saint Nicholas (in Italian, San Nicola), to whom they directed their prayers in the hope that he might intervene for them as well.

Two successive moments from a miracle of the saintly bishop are painted in the cusps of the wings of an altar piece by Bernardo Daddi (active between 1312 and 1348).[29] On the left, with the wings open, Saint Nicholas frees the child Adeodato; on the right, he restores him to his parents (figs. 111–12). Adeodato had been captured by "Saracens,"[30] and taken as a slave to their king. A year passed. On the saint's feast day, the lad, who was serving at table and had a precious cup in his hand, suddenly remembered how elaborately his parents had been used to celebrate Saint

Figures 111–112. *Saint Nicholas Frees Adeodato from Servitude to the Pagan King* (left); *The Saint Restores Adeodato to His Parents* (right). Bernardo Daddi, wings of a small altarpiece, tempera panel, 1336. Siena, Pinacoteca Nazionale.

Nicholas's day, and burst into tears.[31] The king, upon learning the cause of the child's despair, grew angry: "Whatever your Nicholas may do," he said, "you will remain here with us!" On the instant a terrible wind destroyed the palace and Adeodato, still holding the cup in his hand, found himself in front of the chapel where his parents were celebrating the feast of Saint Nicholas.

In the wing on the left (fig. 111) the king is wearing a turban and clutching a menacing knife as he turns toward the saint, who has grabbed the lad by his hair to steal him back from his captors. Adeodato is a little off balance, caught by surprise. The only dinner guest, sitting beside the king, is a pretty young girl, without the band round her neck and the veil over her hair that were typical of married women. Was this a way to hint that the "Saracens" indulged in shameless behavior? In the wing on the right (fig. 112), the parents of Adeodato (the mother wearing the band and the veil) are at table with a religious, suggesting the pious atmosphere of the meal. Their gestures express joy and amazement; on the table there is no sign of a knife. The painter constructed the two scenes following an identical schema so that the comparison and the contrast would be immediate. The fabric that rises to a considerable height in the cusp on the left is trimmed with a rich gilded border; in the cusp on the right, the fabric does not rise nearly as high, leaving the walls of the city visible: this single differentiating detail is charged with significance. On the left the uniformly golden sky indicates exile from home, and foreignness; on the right the city walls, though barely delineated, express with great immediacy the comfort of protection, the return "home," to one's family and native place.[32]

Saint Nicholas, the great protector of infancy, was even capable of battling and winning against demonic infanticide, in a miracle that perhaps originates as compensatory reaction to a real case of child-snatching that ended badly. It concerns a father

who solemnly celebrated the feast of Saint Nicholas every year out of love for his son, who was then learning Latin. On one occasion the father prepared a banquet, to which he invited numerous clerics. But the devil came to the door, dressed as a pilgrim and asking for alms; the father immediately sent his son to give them. The boy went, but found the pilgrim gone, so he ran after him. But when he got to a fork in the path, the devil seized him and strangled him. When the father was told, he was desperate; taking the body, he laid it on the bed, and cried out in pain: "O my beloved son, what has become of you? O Saint Nicholas, is this the reward for all the honor I have always paid you?" And as he spoke those words, the boy, as though awaking from a deep sleep, opened his eyes and got up.[33]

As painted by Ambrogio Lorenzetti (fig. 113), the story takes place in a two-story house, with the narrative beginning on the upper floor. This allows the painter to unfold the sequence by guiding the eye of the observer down the stairs to the ground floor, where the miracle occurs, with a brilliantly conceived corkscrew motion. At the same time the characters are made to advance and recede through the perspective plane: on the upper story their alignment leads from the depth of the room to the foreground; then they descend the winding stairs; the action shifts to the foreground space in front of the bedchamber; and finally they recede back into the dimness of the interior in the scene of the boy returning to life on the bed. In the banquet room Ambrogio has placed three servants in strategic locations: the first, leaning against the wall that separates the room from the stairway, leads the gaze of the viewer to abandon the banquet, as the boy at the top of the stairs is doing. The second, entering through the door at the rear, turns round to address a third colleague, who is barely visible in the room behind, suggesting an extension of space beyond the reach of the viewer's eye. The sense of depth is augmented still further by the daring foreshortening of the L-shaped table, and the slight tilt that places the viewer below it, looking up.

The boy descends to give the alms to the false pilgrim, who reappears beyond the staircase (a way of indicating space that continues out past the reach of the viewer's

Figure 113. *A Child Brought Back to Life by Saint Nicholas.* Ambrogio Lorenzetti, panel, c. 1332, from a larger work, now lost, in the Church of San Procolo at Florence. Florence, Uffizi. Scala / Art Resource, NY.

eye) in the act of strangling the boy with his clawed hands. The story then moves back from left to right, to the bedchamber, where the dead child is first mourned by his parents, and then, as if in slow-motion cinematography, comes back to life and gets to his feet to the amazement of his parents and their friends. The vivifying rays that stream from the mouth and hand of Saint Nicholas, who is suspended in midair on the left, reach the head of the child lying on the bed through an open window. They trace a line perpendicular to that of the elbow-shaped staircase, dividing the upper story, occupied by the relatives and clerics enjoying their banquet, from the ground floor, the place of the miracle. The intricate visual movements that Ambrogio has organized force the gaze of the viewer to dwell on the details of a rich medieval house: the staircase, rather than simply being made of wood, is entirely built of stone and is largely sheltered by a porch roof supported by slender columns. The same roof covers the veranda-balcony, which has a carved corbel. The rooms on the other hand have ceilings with exposed beams, and are very small: the one downstairs is practically filled by the large bed (the bedcover has a "plaid" pattern), and the ever present long low chests that flank it, and in the one upstairs the table takes up most of the space, even though the guests are not excessively numerous.

Chapter Five

Childhood Learning

In many families the children would never have learned to read at any age, and—since reading and writing were not automatically taught together, as they are today—even fewer would have learned to read and write. But in a merchant family of the fourteenth century, not only did the husband have to know how to work with pen in hand, but his wife was in every likelihood literate as well, so she could manage things when her husband was away, which he might be for extended periods.

In his parents' arms, the child would begin by learning to recognize the letters of the alphabet carved into pieces of fruit, and when he learned to identify them, he would receive the "support" itself to munch, as a reward. This technique was widely employed, and Buffalmacco refers to it in the novella we looked at previously from the *Decameron*, once again to deride Maestro Simone with flattery about his claim to learning: "My dear doctor, it is quite clear you have been to Bologna and have brought back with you to this city a pair of well-sealed lips; and let me tell you more. You are not the type who learned his ABCs on an apple, as many dunces do, no sir, you learned them on a much longer fruit, the melon."[1] That an apple was once a compelling reward—what child would feel this way today?—reminds us of the remoteness of the Middle Ages, the mutability of the things children value, the disappearance of little everyday desires.

In families with more means, there were "educational toys," such as, for example, an alphabet wheel in gesso that miraculously survives, perhaps from the fourteenth century (fig. 114), or a covered pewter cup, likewise from the fourteenth century, decorated with the entire

alphabet; the letter *A*, the first the child would pronounce, is on the knob (fig. 115). Handling and touching things, putting them in one's mouth, all the ways of getting to know the world were associated with visual memory in the early acquisition of reading skills.[2] We find out about the instruction of children primarily from images portraying family life either within the restricted nuclear family of Jesus, or within the *Santa parentela*, his extended lineage. Mary, as his mother, is also his first teacher. We see her in a panel of the fifteenth century[3] (fig. 116) lifting her gaze from the missal opened to the pages of the Magnificat (the words with which she accepts the news that she will be the mother of God) to observe her son, who holds in his hand a tablet shaped like a cutting board, with a chalk surface supporting script, the lines of which he is following with the finger of his right hand so as not to lose his place. It consists of letters of the alphabet and syllables formed by a single consonant repeated in conjunction with each of the vowels, "ba, be, bi, bo, bu," (fig. 116, detail), an interesting detail that reveals a precise method of teaching. In a panel dating to around

Figure 114. Alphabet wheel in gesso. Fourteenth century (?). Paris, Saint-Denis, Unité d'archeologie.

Figure 115. Cup with the alphabet. Pewter, fourteenth century. London, Victoria and Albert Museum.

Figure 116. *The Baby Jesus Learns to Read under the Guidance of the Madonna*. Master of Borsigliana (Pietro da Talada?), tempera panel, fifteenth century. Capraia di Sillico (Pieve Fosciana, Lucca), Church of S. Maria.

1335, with scenes from the *Life of the Virgin*, Mary's role is reversed, for now it is she who is learning to read from a Psalter while her mother, Anna, at her shoulder, shows her the line to spell out: it is an appropriate one, an invitation from Psalms to submit to the divine will. While learning to read, Mary learns her own destiny at the same time: "Listen, daughter, look, pay careful attention: forget your nation and the house of your father, for the king will fall in love with your beauty, since he is the Lord your God."[4]

In a page from a manuscript that mothers especially must have gazed on with trust (fig. 117), the words "Saint Anna, pray for us" ("Sancta Anna ora pro nobis") frame the image of a very affectionate mother-daughter relationship: Anna bends over to embrace Mary and, using a little pointed wand, helps her to read a line of the Psalter, which this time is opened to Psalm 24, of which we can recognize the first words of verse 2, "Deus meus in te confido" ("O my God I rely on you"), an invocation to God to pardon the misdeeds of youth.[5]

Even the "cousins" of Jesus are good little children: in the central panel of a triptych by Quentin Metsys from the fifteenth century dedicated to the *Santa Parentela*,[6] Mary is at the center with the Child, who is playing with a robin, to one of whose feet he has tied a thread; Saint Anna offers a cluster of grapes to her grandson, and flanking are the two Marys, Mary Salome and Mary Clopas, with their children. Mary Clopas sits on the left, serving as a reading stand for her two oldest children, who have placed on her knee a manuscript which they are carefully leafing through. At her feet is the smallest child, who does not yet know how to read: a manuscript lies upside down on his legs. He is intent on observing a figurine and is surrounded by illustrated books and cushions that have instructive images embroidered on them.

Learning to read meant both learning a new language, Latin, and undergoing religious instruction. The psalms were memorized aloud to facilitate word acquisition:[7] children's drills consisted of letters printed one by one or in groups of syllables on little tablets coated with chalk or wax, but then with the Psalter in front of them their memory prompted them to recognize whole words. (In terms of modern North American pedagogy, this method was obviously much closer to "phonics" than it was to "whole language," but Italian pedagogy contrasts a method in which the child learns the alphabet and then interprets new words letter by letter, with a "global method" in which the child construes new words syllable by syllable, and it is a medieval version of the latter that we see employed in some of the images discussed here.) Two other prayers basic to the life of a good Christian, the Lord's Prayer (Pater noster) and Hail Mary (Ave Maria), were often written on tablets and recited from memory, for they had the advantages of being brief and containing almost all the letters of

Figure 117. *Saint Anna Teaches the Virgin to Read.* Miniature, fourteenth century. Paris, Bibliothèque Nationale, MS Fr. 400, fol. 38v.

the alphabet. Moreover, children would have been impressed to learn that the Lord's Prayer had been composed by God "with his own mouth," and the "the angel Gabriel had pronounced the Hail Mary to the blessed Virgin."[8] In a manuscript page of 1355–1356, from a miscellaneous codex that contains, amongst other things, a "Bible of the poor,"[9] there is recounted, in words and images, the edifying story of an anonymous baby girl, the daughter of nobility and a future saint: "Here the five-year-old girl is instructed in the alphabet and after that in the Psalter." We see her at her teacher's side, with the tablet on which we can make out the alphabet and the Lord's Prayer, and then later, when she has grown a bit, reading together with the teacher's assistant (fig. 118).[10] The girl had a great passion for the Baby Jesus, and often used to play with him. Once Jesus asked her, "How much do you love me?" She answered precipitously that she loved him as much as she loved her own dress, but then regretted her own vanity and corrected herself, saying, "No, I

Figure 118. *A Girl Learns to Read with a Little Tablet and a Psalter.* Drawing, fourteenth century, from the *Krumauer Bilder Codex.* Vienna, Österreichische Nationalbibliothek, MS 370, fol. 131r.

Figure 119. *La Virtù della Grammatica* (*The Virtue of Grammar*). Fresco, beginning of the fifteenth century. Foligno (Perugia), Palazzo Trinci, Sala delle Arti Liberali e dei Pianeti. Now attributed to Gentile da Fabriano.

love you like my own heart." But the excessive love the little girl felt for Jesus overwhelmed her heart. The women who were preparing her tiny corpse saw that on the
breast of the dead girl there had appeared, written in gold, the phrase "I love you
like my own heart," a prize both learned and ingenuous—letters of gold!—that
rewarded the little girl's aptitude for learning.[11]

The alphabet is paired with the Hail Mary on a page of a manuscript that a boy is
reading, with the help of a stylus[12] in a fresco of Palazzo Trinci at Foligno from the
beginning of the fifteenth century (fig. 119): he and a beautiful young woman who
guides him, clasping the wrist of his hand as it follows the lines, together form the

Figure 120. *The Ages of Man.*
Miniature, fifteenth century,
from Bartholomeus Anglicus,
On the properties of things (*De
proprietatibus rerum*). Paris,
Bibliothèque Nationale, MS
Fr. 135, fol. 193. Childhood
is symbolized by an adult
thrashing a boy with a rod.

image of *Gramatica* (Grammar). The fresco breathes an
air of great calm, and the Virtue is without the attribute that usually accompanies her: the rod, held to be an
indispensable aid to learning.

Even Jesus, when he was a boy, had been given a
good whack at school, according to the apocryphal
gospels, for the master, ignorant of who his pupil actually was, could not accept the idea that a student should
trace out the letters alpha and omega on his tablet,
in other words, that he should be so presumptuous as to believe himself to be the
beginning and the end of everything.[13] Physical punishment of children was such an
everyday occurrence that, to represent *Childhood* in a miniature depicting the *Ages of
Man*, the artist had recourse to a scene of an adult thrashing a child (fig. 120). For
Boccaccio, too, the most obvious simile to use in characterizing sobbing is a child's
reaction to being beaten. The father of the unhappy Ghismunda, before giving way
to his anger, grows tender for a moment and admits the possibility of forgiveness:
"Having said this, he lowered his head and wept like a child who has been severely
beaten."[14]

Brutal and abusive forms of discipline were used. Guibert of Nogent (who died around 1124) could recall them.

Once I had been beaten in class; the class was in fact no more than a room of our house. For my teacher had given up the job of teaching the other students he had formerly taught in order to concentrate on me alone. My mother had prudently demanded that, in return for an increased salary and more honorable conditions. So when that day's lessons were over, at around the hour of vespers, I had gone to sit at my mother's knee, having been pretty badly struck, more so than I deserved. My mother, as usual, began to ask me whether or not I had been beaten that day, and I categorically denied it, not wishing to seem to inform against my teacher; but she overrode my objections, and, lifting my undergarment, which is called a *subucula*, or indeed a *chemise*, she saw that my little arms were covered with bruises, and that on my back the skin was swollen all over on account of the blows of the rod. After she had lamented the excessive savagery inflicted on one so young, upset and agitated, with her eyes full of tears, she said to me, "You are no longer going to become a cleric, nor will you any longer suffer these pains for the sake of learning Latin." But I replied, looking at her with all the severity I could muster, "Even if it costs me my life, I will not desist from learning Latin and becoming a cleric."[15]

The author of this memoir was a monk, one well satisfied with his own childhood self, or with that self as he imagined it: bright (too bright to have deserved that much punishment), full of courage and determination. Be that as it may, however, Guibert of Nogent was describing a typical situation: learning and being thrashed were one and the same thing. When pupil and master are apes, the event may seem ridiculous: the little apes busy reading manuscripts and writing on their tablets, the teacher-ape busy being a teacher, in other words, beating an awkward student with a bundle of rods (fig. 121). Yet the animal disguise perhaps masks a certain uneasiness, maybe even a genuine protest, however controlled and light-hearted. Sometimes it went beyond a joke: we have already read about the fire in the monastery of Saint Gallen.[16] At the time of the persecution of Christians, the styluses of the pupils of San Cassiano of Imola, a teacher in a small school, actually became the instruments of his martyrdom. The illuminator of the ninth century who depicted the ferocity of the revolt was also expressing repressed childhood urges,[17] aroused perhaps by some sentence dictated to him by his own teacher, along the lines of "If you don't write well I will beat you on the back," or "Write, child, don't be distracted and don't play around. Learn on the tablet so as to be able to write on parchment later, 'I am an ass who doesn't know how to write.'" Here, though, the source of the thought is clearly the student himself: "I hope my teacher breaks his legs!"[18]

aulle · et tu   li fiftes · et or Anon maiftre telles
nes · fi que   et or les cheuex gaunes come

Figure 121. *The School of Monkeys.* Miniature, thirteenth century, from Robert de Borron, *L'Histoire du Graal.* Paris, Bibliothèque Nationale, MS Fr. 95, fol. 355. Apes learn to read, with a teacher beating a student.

After learning to read, children progressed to the study of mathematics, learning arithmetic and solving problems; the cases with which they were presented were much like the ones that tormented our own childhood: once a boy was mortally bitten by a snake, and his mother asked him: "My son, if you were to live for as long as you have been alive to this point, and then that much again, and then half that much again, how long would you have lived, all told?" Or else: "Three brothers each have one sister; the six of them arrive at a river crossing, but the boat available can only hold two people. Decorum requires that each sister cross with her brother. How did they do it?"[19] For arithmetic children used the abacus, a horizontal board with columns for the numbers that aided them in multiplication and division. Or else, as the monk Hugo of Saint Victor recalls, they used stones and bits of coal; the latter was especially useful for drawing geometric figures on the pavement.[20]

Chapter Six

ADULT READING

L ittle girls went to school, too; but more often they passed their time preparing themselves to become good housekeepers and good wives: learning to spin, embroider, weave, knit, and sew (figs. 122–123). Boccaccio, in the prologue to the *Decameron* (in which seven of the tale-tellers are women, and only three are men), states that he thought of women as his ideal readership—the ones who knew how to read, of course, while "to those others who are not I leave the needle, spindle, and wool winder" (fig. 123).[1] The lives of his women readers are "restricted by the wishes, whims, and commands of fathers, mothers, brothers, and husbands, they remain most of the time limited to the narrow confines of their bedrooms, where they sit in apparent idleness, now wishing one thing and now wishing another, turning over in their minds a number of thoughts which cannot always be pleasant ones." They are obliged to put up with this restless discontent, unlike men, who, if they "are afflicted by melancholy or ponderous thoughts, have many ways of alleviating or forgetting them: if they wish, they can take a walk and listen to or look at many different things; they can go hawking, hunting, or fishing; they can ride, gamble, or attend to business. Each of these pursuits has the power, either completely or in part, to occupy a man's mind and to remove from it a painful thought, even if for only a brief moment; and so, in one way or another, either consolation follows or the pain becomes less."[2]

Women read to entertain themselves or for the purpose of prayer. They used reading stands made for the men of the house (it is difficult to imagine that they were built to meet the particular needs of

Figure 122. *The Little Embroiderers*. Detail from the altarpiece of the Virgin and Saint George, panel, fifteenth century. Villafranca del Panadés, Barcelona.

Figure 123. *Spinning Yarn with a Spinning Machine and Carding Wool*. Miniature, c. 1470, from G. Boccaccio, *Des clères et nobles femmes*. New York, New York Public Library, Spencer Collection, MS 33, fol. 56r. In the foreground is an *arcolaio*, a revolving wool winder.

Figure 124. *A Woman Intent on Reading*. Miniature, fifteenth century, from G. Boccaccio, *Le livre des clères et nobles femmes*. Paris, Bibliothèque Nationale, MS Fr. 599, fol. 22r. Her reading stand has a tubular compartment to hold rolls of unbound parchment.

women), of various shapes that reveal the attention devoted to improving this type of object. With her back turned to a fireplace where a glowing fire hisses, the woman in this miniature (fig. 124) has placed her book on a wall-mounted reading stand that can be adjusted as the light source shifts. She is savoring a moment of serenity and peace in the warm and silent room.

Figure 125. *Santa Barbara Reading*.
Master of Flemalle (Robert Campin),
oil panel, 1438. Madrid, Prado.

Figure 126. *An Adulterous Encounter*.
Miniature, late fourteenth century,
from Boccaccio, *Decameron* 8.8. Vienna,
Österreichische Nationalbibliothek,
MS 2561, fol. 304v.

Saint Barbara also reads her book of prayers with her back turned to a burning fire (fig. 125). The embers and the pieces of wood are held in place by two andirons of wrought iron. She has placed a white cloth between the manuscript and her hands to avoid spoiling it and staining the cover. We are in a luxurious room at the beginning of the fifteenth century. The bench on which Barbara is sitting is provided with a footrest, and is made more comfortable by cushions and drapery covers. The bench also has an ingenious adjustable backrest, so that the angle of recline can be changed at will. Even the candleholder on the mantel of the fireplace can be swiveled. When the candle is lit, it will render homage to the statuette placed above it on the shelf of the mantelpiece, which represents the Trinity as divine paternity. Much detailed thought has been given to putting those who dwell here at ease. A pitcher and a bronze basin have been placed on the finely carved sideboard; above, a well-ironed white towel is ready, hanging from a pole. Someone has placed a pewter vase holding large, fragrant blue irises on a folding seat. On the shelf beside the fireplace a bottle of transparent glass contains white wine, through which the light streaming through the large glass windows shines: the whole painting almost seems like a hymn to the sensory pleasures of domestic intimacy. It has been left very much up to the initiative of another couple to find comfort and cheer in their surroundings (fig. 126): their bench does indeed have an adjustable backrest, but only one cushion; there is a fireplace with a rack, but is it lit? Will the shuttered windows be glazed? It is probably cold in this small room; a red fabric has been hung on the rear wall as a defense against currents of air and humidity, but it does not reach the ceiling. Clearly, resources were stretched to the limit here.

For reading in the evening or when the weather was bad, a lantern was necessary, attached above the reading stand with a system of arms and brackets. Giovanni da Milano has imagined the Madonna receiving the angelic Annunciation seated in an inlaid high-backed chair, with a table in front of her on which is mounted a complicated rotatable reading stand, a pyramid set on a circle on which a series of volumes is propped (fig. 127). One of them is open and opportunely illuminated by a hanging lamp, which can also be swiveled so that we too can read the response it suggests to the Virgin: "I am the handmaid of the Lord, let what you have said be done to me" (Luke 1:38).

With advancing years the oil lamp no longer sufficed. Luckily, toward the end of the thirteenth century, eyeglasses were invented. "It is not yet twenty years since they discovered the art of making eyeglasses, which let one see clearly, which is one of the finest and most necessary arts the world has, and it is such a short time since they were discovered: a new art, that never was before," says Giordano da Pisa in a sermon at Florence in 1305.[3] Tommaso da Modena, who in 1352 painted forty illustrious members of the Dominican order in the Chapter of San Nicolò in Treviso,

portrayed one of them, Cardinal Hugo of Provence, while writing at a table surrounded by codices: on his nose he has placed a fine pince-nez, which can be folded up (fig. 128).

It was certainly an extraordinary invention, and we can understand the enthusiasm of the learned preacher, for those who dedicated themselves to reading and writing were gradually excluded from intellectual work as they grew older, although they could still rely on their own special personal library, and their memory, a

Figure 127. *The Annunciation.* Giovanni da Milano, central compartment of the predella of the polyptych *Madonna con il Bambino, santi, storie della loro vita e storie evangeliche,* tempera panel, c. 1354. Prato, Pinacoteca Comunale.

Figure 128. *Cardinal Hugo of Provence.* Tommaso da Modena, fresco, 1352. Treviso, Capitolo di San Nicolò. Scala / Art Resource, NY.

faculty that was exercised much more then than it is today. But even men and women engaged in simpler occupations, like manual labor, were disabled by advancing age. When Boccaccio delineates the physical and moral profile of a go-between who assists a young wife to betray her husband, the portrait that results is not a pretty one: yet her continual, and hypocritical, round of visits to churches to gain indulgences (she "constantly went about with her rosary beads in her hand, attending every general indulgence service and talking about nothing but the lives of the Holy Church Fathers and the stigmata of Saint Francis"), and her continual round of visits to houses where she provides shameful favors, are both connected to the fact that she has become an old woman: no longer attractive, no longer an object of desire, but also deprived of any functional role in the house, and consequently poor and marginalized.

> And what the devil are we women good for when we are old anyway, only to sit around the fire and stare at the ashes? . . . when I see myself reduced to the state in which you see me now, where no one would even deign to let me light a rag, only God knows the agony I feel . . . For as you can see, when we get old, no husband or anyone else cares to look at us; on the contrary, we are chased into the kitchen to tell stories to the cat or to count the pots and pans . . . Just show me the man you want , and then leave everything up to me; but let me remind you of one thing, my child: I am a poor woman who needs looking after, and from now on I want you to have a share in all my indulgences and in as many Our Fathers as I recite, so that God may look kindly upon your dearly departed.

For her trouble the old woman will receive a meager reward, "a piece of salted meat."[4]

Chapter Seven

INDOORS

T oday it is a simple matter to start a fire and extinguish it. In the Middle Ages, however, it took a lot of ability and patience to get a fire going: you had to have good dry tinder, which required long and patient preparation,[1] strike the flint against the steel and be ready to catch the spark,[2] keep it going by blowing on it through a hollow reed (fig. 129);[3] and then, when the fire was going, keep adding wood and make sure there was a proper draft. If you were unlucky and it went out, rather than start all over again, women preferred to go next door to the neighbor's and ask if they could light a rag at their fire:—to ask to borrow some fire, in fact, the way we might ask to borrow a cup of sugar. For this and other reasons it was necessary to have a network of good relationships: the old go-between whom we met a few moments ago says, to illustrate how marginalized she is, "no one would even deign to let me light a rag."[4] A woman with a bucket in her hand and fire tongs that are gripping a burning ember represents the *Sower of Discord* in one of the twelve proverbs painted by Pieter Brueghel the Elder in 1558, which carries the inscription, "I carry fire in one hand, water in the other, and pass my time with gossip and little women." These details are of interest because they show how, the passage of centuries notwithstanding, the provision of water and the request for help from the neighbors to get the fire going remained two of the most habitual tasks of women (fig. 130).[5]

In the evening you had to be careful to cover the coals thoroughly with ash so that they would still be live the next morning and so that they did not start a fire when no one was awake (fig. 131). Like those

Figure 129. *A Devil Fans the Flames with a Tube*. Andrea Bonaiuti, detail of a fresco, fourteenth century. Florence, Santa Maria Novella, Cappellone degli Spagnoli.

Figure 130. *The Sower of Discord*. Pieter Brueghel the Elder, detail from *Twelve Flemish Proverbs*, oil on panel, 1558. Antwerp, Museum Mayer van den Bergh.

Figure 131. *Houses Burning*. Ambrogio Lorenzetti, detail from *Bad Government. The Effects in the Countryside* (*Il Mal Governo. Gli effetti in campagna*), fresco, 1338–1339. Siena, Palazzo Pubblico, Sala della Pace. Scala / Art Resource, NY.

children who are so full of energy that when you try to restrain them they break free and hurl themselves all over the room, the flames in the fireplace were always ready with their darting tongues and bursting sparks to transform the house into a heap of cinders.

To get ready to go to bed was not a simple matter, either. There were a lot of precautions to take. Let us listen to the wise counsels of the "householder of Paris" to his young wife: "When Madame Agnes the beguine or Master Jean the steward have told you that the fire has been covered in all the chimneys, then you can go ahead and dismiss your servants, to take the rest they need. First, though, check to be sure that each has placed the candleholder with the large base well away from their bed. You also ought, as a precaution, to inculcate in your servitors the habit of snuffing out the candles, by blowing or pinching it just before they get into bed, and not when they are still wearing their chemise."[6] People did in fact sleep entirely unclothed.

The causes of fire were extremely varied, above all, the fact that the houses were built mostly of wood.[7] Also, they stood very close together, with the distance between the facades reduced even more, to the point where they were practically conjoined, by the projecting overhangs, which were also almost completely wooden. In the cities, stalls, granaries, haymows, and straw piles flanked the houses: Sercambi recalls that right near the Cathedral of Siena there stood a haymow.[8] Some activities were particularly dangerous, either because the artisans, like wool workers and rope makers, handled materials that could easily catch fire, or because they needed fire for their work, like, for example, bakers, spice and drug dealers, smiths, nail makers, potters: most of the dishware in domestic use was made of clay fired in furnaces, and roof and gutter tiles were made of clay, too. Sometimes fires that were lit in exultation on the tops of towers would get out of control, fanned by the wind,[9] or else a lit candle or lamp left unattended, perilous but irreplaceable sources of nighttime illumination, might be the source. At Siena the commune instituted a corps of fire fighters, and also had a policy of paying reimbursement for the damage to burned houses, except for the damage done to the house in which the fire had originated.[10] Those who deliberately set fires could expect to burn at the stake, for the authorities feared fire on account of the damage to persons and property, but also because they were a focus and expression of social revolt: "It happens repeatedly that a few vile persons who possess nothing, burn and set fires in the huts, heaps of grain, straw stacks and crops, and other things belonging to citizens and peasants, saying, 'We have nothing to lose.'"[11]

As we read the extensive minutes of the council meetings, we encounter, one after another, collapsed buildings, damage, and persons burned to death in fires or dying later from the burns they received. In 1302, for example, "a major fire broke

out in the houses of the Saracini and the Scotti and lasted two days and two nights
. . . and the commune reimbursed [the cost of] . . . a number of houses and galleries
that were burned." A particularly dramatic fire occurred in 1413, caused by a wool
worker who had worked all night and, perhaps because he was tired, had let fall "a
light into the tow [fiber ready for spinning], and he couldn't put it out, and a lot of
things were burned, and six persons who went in to try to save things died in the fire
because the flooring and the stairs collapsed under them, and they fell into the fire
and were burned and died. Golla, the master carpenter, was left straddling a beam,
and was only rescued with difficulty, and he was burned all over, and he lived about
twenty days and then he too died from the burns."[12] The authorities tried to keep
the most dangerous activities, like that of the charcoal burners, at a distance from
the city. Artisans who needed water for their work and furnaces too, like the "cop-
pai" and "orciolai" (terms for makers of terra cotta oil jars), set up shop near the
water fountains, or requested the installation of new ones, because they needed
them for their industrial processes, but also because of the danger of fire, "which
God forfend." It is easy to see how Boccaccio's artful Fra Cipolla could fool his
unsophisticated audience by offering them, in return for generous contributions,
the potent talisman of the coals of San Lorenzo.[13] So great was their desire to
acquire protection against the flames that none of them paid any attention to the

Figure 132. *Santa Marta in the Kitchen.*
Giovanni di Corraduccio, fresco,
beginning of the fifteenth century.
Foligno, Convento di Sant'Anna,
old refectory.

mocking words with which Fra Cipolla ended: "whoever makes the sign of the cross on himself with this charcoal will live for one year safe in the knowledge that he will not be cooked by fire without his feeling it."[14] Inside the houses people were always alert to the risk, and whenever possible—that is, if they had money to spend and the house had several stories—they located the kitchen directly under the roof, precisely to prevent an outbreak of fire on the ground floor from spreading to the upper floors and burning down the whole house (fig. 132). The protagonist of a novella of Sacchetti, Ferrantino degli Argenti, after getting caught in a sudden rainstorm, wore himself out climbing up and down sets of stairs: "Sticking his head in one door after another, and climbing the stairs, he went about poking into other people's houses and brazenly trying to find a fire at which to dry himself off. Going from one to another, by chance he came upon a door, entered, and went up. In the kitchen he found a large fire with two full pots, and a spit of capons and partridges, and a beautiful young servant girl who was turning them while they roasted."[15]

At Palazzo Davanzati the kitchen on the top floor has been preserved, and with it the consternation that someone registered on the wall, with charcoal, when the news spread, amid the clatter of pots and spits, of the murder of Giuliano de' Medici: "1478. On 26 April Giuliano de' Medici was killed in Santa Maria de' Fiore" (fig. 133).[16] Locating the kitchen at the top of the house entailed a high cost in labor, since everything—wood, water, food supplies—had to be carried up the steep stairs by hand (fig. 134). Hence we shouldn't assume that raw foodstuffs, or dishes, or peoples' hands were always being washed or that fresh water was used every time they were washed, for a bucket of water had to last a long time, and thus, though no one realized the connection, diseases and epidemics lasted a long time, too.

When comfortably well-off people gathered socially, one of the servants went round at the beginning of the meal, and then repeatedly between courses, with an *aquamanile* (literally, "hand-waterer"), a pitcher customarily shaped like an animal or

Figure 133. *Inscription with the News of the Murder of Giuliano de' Medici.* Florence, Palazzo Davanzati, third floor, kitchen.

Figure 134. *Staircase in Palazzo Davanzati*. Fourteenth century. Florence, Palazzo Davanzati. The lowest flight of steps acts as a flying buttress. Scala / Art Resource, NY.

<small>✤ Figure 135. *The Judgment of Pilate.*
Miniature, c. 1230, from the
Psalter of Bonmont. Besançon,
Bibliothèque Muncipale, MS
54, fol. 11v.

Figure 136. *Acquamanile* in the
shape of a unicorn. Cast bronze,
end of the fourteenth century.
Paris, Musée de Cluny.</small>

a dragon: "After water was provided for their hands, the steward, following the
Queen's wishes, sat them all at the table, where, once the food was served, they ate
happily." Thus do the party of friends of the *Decameron* enjoy the pause before the
tales of the ninth day.[17] Even Pontius Pilate does not hesitate to "wash his hands" in
front of Christ, cleaning them under an *aquamanile* in the form of a dragon offered to
him by a servant (figs. 135–136).

At Palazzo Davanzati one could draw water from the gallery on each floor through
a window that gave access to the wellhead (fig. 137), but that was an uncommon solu-
tion, one available only to particularly wealthy people. Having a private well, even
without such an ingenious system, was a luxury that spread, in the Trecento, only in

Figure 137. One of the small
windows that allowed water to
be drawn from the well to each
floor of Palazzo Davanzati.
Florence, Palazzo Davanzati.

Figure 138. *A Woman Washing
Dishes beside the Sea.* Miniature,
late fourteenth century, from
Boccaccio, *Decameron* 2.4.
Paris, Bibliothèque de l'Arse-
nal, MS 5070, fol. 51v.
Scala / Art Resource, NY.

lordly residences. Throughout this period, gutters for draining rainwater from the roofs into the street or into a cistern were rare, and for that reason doors and windows had to be protected from the driving rain with little supplementary shelters. Private wells often yielded foul-smelling water, which in our world would be labeled nonpotable. Only women who lived near the seaside had an alternative: when Landolfo Rufolo made it to shore after a shipwreck, the first thing he saw was "a poor little woman" who "was washing her dishes with the sand and the salt water, and making them gleam" (fig. 138).

Normally one went to the communal well (fig. 139) in the piazza or the crossroads of the neighborhood:[18] an opportunity to meet, exchange news, enjoy a pleasant conversation, and wait one's turn to lower the bucket, but for which one paid dearly while staggering home with the heavy weight pressing on one's shoulders, making it hard to breathe.

Figure 139. *Monna Ghita Pretends to Throw Herself into a Well, But Actually Throws in a Stone.* Miniature, late fourteenth century, from Boccaccio, *Decameron* 7.4. Paris, Bibliothèque de l'Arsenal, MS 5070, fol. 252r.

The flow of water through the public conduits was tightly controlled: at Siena only the *stufe* (the public baths), the laundries, and the inns were permitted to draw from them directly, but at the beginning of the fifteenth century the permissions were withdrawn because of numerous infractions, for it was found that private citizens had made "finestre" (windows) and

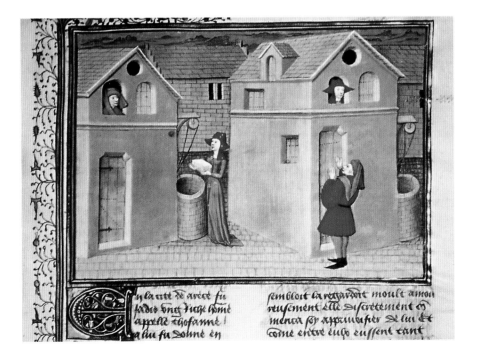

"usci" (entrances) in the conduits "and were washing their clothes in them and dumping other filth, with the result that fountains and the water supply were being spoiled."[19] Another way the Sienese got the most use out of their water was to construct fountains with three connected basins: the first supplied the locals with their water, the second, which captured the overflow from the first, served as a drinking trough for animals, and the third, which captured the overflow from the second, was reserved for use by the women as a washbasin.[20]

Water and fire, which cost so much effort to provide, are described as the foremost source of pleasure in the list of domestic delights that a husband expected. The "householder of Paris" writes

> With men lies the care and the duty of attending to business outside the house, and that is what husbands must be thinking about, and come and go and run here and there in rain, wind, snow, and hail; now soaked, now dry; now sweating, now shivering; badly fed, badly lodged, badly shod, sleeping in rotten beds—and a husband withstands all of this because he takes strength from the expectation of the fuss his wife will make over him when he gets home, the ease and joy and pleasure she will provide him or see that others provide him with: to have his shoes removed before a good fire, to have his feet washed, to have fresh shoes and stockings brought, to eat and drink well, to be served and honored, to go to bed between white sheets with a white bonnet, well covered with good furs, and made content by other secret joys and delights, intimacies and amours, which I will pass over in silence. And the next morning, fresh underwear and clothing.[21]

On a warm day there is always real enjoyment in splashing around freely in a pool or a stream, and in the past people must have taken extra pleasure in bathing, knowing how much trouble it took to collect enough water just to fill a bathtub. In one miracle, two young monks who were headed for perdition, since they had decided to leave their monastery, were ultimately made to think again. But before that, as soon as they got outside the oppressive walls of the institution, the first thing they were drawn to was a stream of water (fig. 140),[22] and the illuminator depicts very effectively the joy of their sudden release, as the fugitives, almost disrobed, kick their legs this way and that, gamboling with joy: they can hardly wait to dive back in. Boccaccio's leisurely description of the Valley of the Ladies weaves an enchanting picture out of carefully chosen literary citations; but the "tiny lake, like those which city dwellers sometimes build in their gardens to use as a fishpond if they have the means to do so" which is shown to the happy group of women of the *Decameron* deep in a hilly landscape that rolls away into

Figure 140. *Flight and Return to the Monastery of Two Young Monks.* Miniature, 1281–1284, from Alfonso X the Wise, *Cantigas de Santa María.* Florence, Biblioteca Nazionale Centrale, MS B. R. 20, fol. 7r.

the distance, has a different resonance, because it evokes the taste of pleasures that have really been felt by anyone who likes to swim and play in the water. The water in the lake was so pellucid that "its bed clearly showed a stretch of the finest gravel, which could have been counted to the last grain by anyone who had nothing better to do." The swimming party of the seven nude women in the little lake, "which concealed their milk-white bodies not unlike the way a crystal glass conceals a pink rose," ends this brief realistic interlude with an enchanting poetic simile.[23]

It was a simple norm of hygiene for women to wash their hair every Saturday and "rinse away all the dust and grime that have accumulated through the course of the past week's labors,"[24] and if a man was lucky, he might get a couple of women to wash his hair, too (fig. 141). Men and women would also wash themselves all over whenever they felt they had become too smelly or unclean,[25] and newborns were supposed to have a bath three times a day. Seven was the right number according to Marie de France,[26] but that would have been thought an exorbitant practice.

A steaming bath could also offer discrete pleasures, often a prelude to other, more intimate ones. Marchese Azzo VIII of Ferrara was accustomed from time to time to pass the evening, and the night, with a beautiful widow, and when he was coming the woman always prepared a bath and a good dinner. On one occasion she had already got these things ready when the marchese had to change his plans because of an unexpected engagement. "The lady was somewhat displeased, and not knowing what to do with herself, she decided to take the bath drawn for the marchese herself and then to eat and go to bed. And so into the bath she stepped." While she was relaxing in the water, she heard the moans of a young man who was crying and trembling with cold outside the door. It was none other than Rinaldo d'Asti, the merchant devoted to San Giuliano whom we have already met, the one who was the victim of the false merchants in the wood (p. 32 above). Rinaldo was welcomed into the house, "shivering all over," and the woman said to him, "'Quickly my good man, step into this bath, which is still warm.' Without waiting for any further invitation, Rinaldo did so most gladly, and with the heat from the bath reviving his body, he felt as if he had been completely returned from the dead to the living." Dressed in the clothes of the woman's late husband and warmed in a *caminata*, a spacious room with

Figure 141. *Two Girls Wash a Man's Hair*. Miniature, 1390–1400, from the Bible of Wenceslaus. Vienna, Österreichische Nationalbibliothek, MS 2759, fol. 174v.

a large fire, Rinaldo was invited to take supper. "The table was set up" (this was always a provisional piece of furniture, made of a flat board and two sawhorses so that it could be assembled in a moment; fig. 142), and after washing their hands, the young man and the widow began their repast, and their conversation became progressively more gay and frank, to the point that Rinaldo ended up very willingly taking the place of the marchese in bed.[27] On a small matter of daily life: it was such

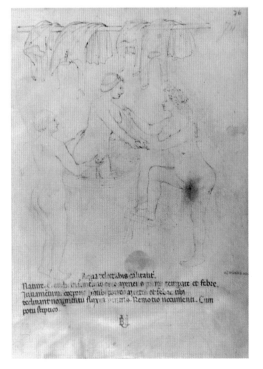

Figure 142. *Banqueting on an Assembled Table.* Miniature, beginning of the fourteenth century. London, British Library, Luttrell Psalter, fol. 208.

Figure 143. *Three Women Take a Bath at Home.* Drawing, c. 1390–1400, from *Tacuinum sanitatis.* Liège, Bibliothèque générale. MS 1041, fol. 76. By Permission of the British Library.

a major undertaking to prepare a steaming bath and such a pleasure to sink into one that in the novella it is presented as absolutely natural not only for the widow not to waste the bath already prepared but also to have someone else use it after her, since it was still hot (fig. 143).[28]

The public baths were the usual place for amorous rendezvous, and the darkness of the bedchamber where a couple would go to lie down, perspiring and languid after emerging from the water, played a trick on an inexperienced and jealous wife, who found herself in bed, without knowing it, with the lover whom up till then she had disdainfully spurned in one of Boccaccio's novellas. An illuminator has thrown an indiscreet light into the room where, surrounded by curtains, the two young people are lying naked in bed beside one another, while a maid brings in two pails of water, hung from a rack on her back, to fill up the tub. This woman has been added either to identify the locale more clearly or to suggest further pleasures to be found in this place of assignation (fig. 144).

In this novella,[29] Boccaccio did not bother to give a description of the public bathhouse, with its rites and its seductions, but he does so in minute detail in another, where the negative protagonist is an avid courtesan. Madonna Jancofiore— for that is her name—aims to get her hands on the riches of the merchant Salabaetto

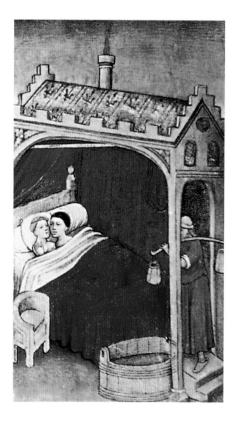

Figure 144. *Ricciardo and Catella at the Public Bathhouse*. Miniature, fifteenth century, from Boccaccio, *Decameron* 3.6. Paris, Bibliothèque de l'Arsenal, MS 5070, fol. 116r.

and pretends to be deeply in love with him. She reserves a room in the public baths and fixes an appointment with the young man there. He, however, arrives first.

> He was not there long before two slave girls arrived, loaded down with things: one balanced a beautiful large cottonwool mattress on her head, while the other was carrying a big basket full of different objects. After setting down the mattress on a bed in one of the private rooms of the bathhouse, they spread over it a pair of the thinnest sheets edged with silk, and then a bedcover of the whitest Cyprian buckram [a very fine linen fabric] and two marvelously embroidered pillows; having done this they undressed, got into the bath, and washed and scrubbed it thoroughly. Nor was it long before the lady with two more slave girls arrived at the bath.[30]

After kisses and declarations of love

> they both entered the bath naked, attended by two of the slave girls. There, without allowing anyone else to lay a hand upon him, the lady herself, taking marvelous care, washed Salabaetto all over using soaps scented with musk and cloves, and then she had herself washed and rubbed down by the slave girls. And when this was done, the slave girls brought two of the whitest and thinnest sheets, from which there arose so strong an odor of roses that everything in the room seemed to be made of roses; having wrapped Salabaetto in one and draped the lady in the other, they lifted both of them up and carried them to the bed made ready for them. And there, when they stopped perspiring, the sheets were removed by the slave girls, and they were left naked between the other sheets. The most beautiful silver perfume bottles appeared from the basket, some full of rosewater, some with water from orange blossoms, others from jasmine blooms, and still others with various kinds of citron extract,[31] and the slave girls sprinkled all these lotions over them; and later on came boxes of confections and bottles of the most precious wines with which they refreshed themselves.[32]

Then the slave girls depart, leaving the two lovers alone and blissful. The presence of the slave girls, who are evidently felt to be no more the human equals of their masters than a cat would be, embarrasses them not a bit. Madonna Jancofiore does not even need to pretend to be slightly perturbed as she strips herself naked before a naked Salabaetto: a sign that their code of shame had thresholds very different from our own, because of the medieval habit of sleeping undressed, in beds that held numbers of persons in forced promiscuity.

At the agreed time the slaves return, and regale Salabaetto and Madonna Jancofiore with other sweets and wines; the two wash their faces and hands with the perfumed waters and then mutually take their leave, but with the intention of rejoining each other soon after, for that evening the young man has been invited to a magnificent dinner at the woman's house. In her bedroom "he could smell a marvelous aroma of oriental wood and cyprian incense birds, and he saw the luxurious bed and the many beautiful gowns hanging from poles.[33] All these things, taken together and separately, made Salabaetto think that she must be a great and rich lady." This impression—that the lady was deeply in love with him and was very well off—was confirmed the next morning when the young man received the gift of "a handsome and stylish little silver belt around his waist with a beautiful purse attached to it."[34]

Let us leave the calculating Jancofiore as she sets her trap for Salabaetto (who will beat her at her own game). In another of the tales, another grasping courtesan, Madonna Fiordaliso, hoodwinks another naive youth named Andreuccio da Perugia by making use of similar lures and flattery. He is brought to a room perfumed with roses and orange flowers, where there is "a very beautiful curtained bed, and many dresses hanging on poles." They sit together "on a chest at the foot of her bed,"[35] and she starts to tell him the story with which she intends, as we would say, to "con" him. Andreuccio falls for the con, staying for dinner and then staying the night in the house of (so he believes) his long-lost sister. When he needs to use the toilet, he is shown a doorway:

> Andreuccio innocently entered the place, and as he did, by chance he happened to step on a plank which was not nailed to the beam it rested on; this overturned the plank, and he with the plank plunged down through the floor. But by the love of God he was spared from hurting himself in the fall, in spite of the height from which he fell; he was, however, completely covered by the filth that filled the place. In order for you to understand better just what took place and what was going to take place, I shall now describe to you the kind of place it was. Andreuccio was in a narrow alley like the kind we often see between two houses; some planks had been nailed on two beams placed between one house and the other, and there was a place to sit down; and the plank which plunged with him to the bottom was precisely one of these supporting planks.

Andreuccio, after calling for a long time for help, "climbed over a small wall which closed that alley from the street"[36] and ran to knock at the front door of the house in which the incident had taken place—but by this time his "sister" had already taken his money, and the servants pretended not to know him.

A miniature in a manuscript of the *Decameron* represents this incident perfectly and gives us a sectional view of a medieval house (fig. 145). Subsequently Andreuccio will have other adventures, with a happy ending; but Boccaccio's description gives us the chance to learn details that are usually judged unseemly by medieval writers and therefore not mentioned, while at the same time brings us face-to-face with the problems of high urban density. The low wall that closed the alley off

Figure 145. *Andreuccio da Perugia Falls into a Narrow Alley.* Miniature, fifteenth century, from Boccaccio, *Decameron* 2.5. Paris, Bibliothèque de l'Arsenal, MS 5070, fol. 54v.

from the street may have retained the pile of ordure itself, but the stink of it and the clouds of insects buzzing around it would have assaulted anyone who passed by. For similar reasons, when Giovanni Villani describes Roman Florence with a medieval slant, his mind turned to the needs of his own time: "Albinus undertook to pave the whole city, which was a noble work, and beauty and cleanliness of the city. . . . Macrinus had the water conduit constructed, with watercourses and arches . . . so that the city would have an abundance of good water to drink, and for washing the city." Under the "chief fortress of the city . . . the water of the river Arno flowed through a tunnel in which a channel had been dug and arches built; and back into the Arno it flowed underground. At every holiday the city was washed clean with water that gushed from that tunnel."[37] Such faith in the marvelous Roman network of drains and water pipes was a response to the vexing problem of keeping the streets, which were clogged with everything imaginable, clean. In the admiring description that the Anonymus Ticinensis gives of his city, Pavia, we do meet the public pigs, fattened on the refuse that they found by foraging in the streets, but also, as a glory of the present state of things, "latrinarum cuniculi" (underground pits for the latrines) and deep underground sewers so that a heavy rainfall would clean the streets and then drain off into the Ticino.[38]

Figure 146. *Maestro Simone on a Toilet at Night, Wearing a Fur-lined Robe.* Miniature, late fourteenth century, from Boccaccio, *Decameron* 8.9. Vienna, Österreichische Nationalbibliothek, MS 2561, fol. 307v.

Figure 147. *Maestro Simone on a Toilet at night, Wearing a fur-lined Robe.* Miniature, late fourteenth century, from Boccaccio, *Decameron* 8.9. Paris, Bibliothèque Nationale, MS Fr. 12421, fol. 355v. The toilet has three holes.

Figure 148. *Toilet Room off the Nuptial Bedchamber with the Walls Frescoed in a Vair Pattern.* Fourteenth century. Florence, Palazzo Davanzati.

Two different kinds of "luogo da sedere" (literally "place for sitting") can be seen in miniatures (figs. 146, 147) illustrating the false bravery of our friend Simone the doctor, who, to show how tough he is describes how he gets out of a warm bed on a cold night: "I'm not sensitive to the cold, and I don't pay any attention to it; whenever I get up during the night to relieve my bodily needs, as men sometimes do, I hardly ever put a thing on except for a fur coat over my doublet."[39] In the first miniature the toilet is clearly an outhouse, in which Simone sits on a simple one-holer, warmly wrapped, in the middle of the night. The second is a more elaborate three-holer with a high-backed seat, and the illuminator has placed Simone on the middle seat, wearing his doctoral robes, no less.

In the houses of the rich, fabrics, and even fabrics lined with fur, covered the walls in an attempt to counteract the cold, humidity, and currents of air of the bitter months. Those who could not permit themselves such luxury had recourse to fake tapestries painted on the wall. In Palazzo Davanzati the walls were extensively painted to look as though they were covered with fabric; but only in the toilet, a small walled room, solidly built, and on that account alone an improvement on the usual standard, did the fresco imitate a lining of vair. There was perhaps some ironic amusement in displaying, with a very private lack of inhibition, such costly, but purely longed-for, opulence in such a location (fig. 148).

In the houses of the poor the walls were entirely bare, and warmth in the bedroom was supplied by the neighboring bodies. Three sisters sleep in the same bed—their father will perhaps content himself with the long chest beside it—in the miracle of Saint Nicholas by Gentile da Fabriano (fig. 149). More than a prodigy, this miracle is also an act of great charity, since the three balls of gold that are tossed into the room by the future saint will save the girls from imminent prostitution, the only recourse the father had been able to think of to meet the threat of extreme indigence.

A betrayed wife with a noble soul performs an equally magnanimous act vis-à-vis her husband's lover, a poor spinner of wool. The lady visits the girl and finds that the latter "lacked everything: she had no wood to burn, no smoked pork, no candle, no oil, no coal; there was only a bed and a bedcover, the spinning machine, and a few domestic utensils." The lady thinks it her duty to preserve her husband, herself, and her children from shame and therefore requests complicit silence; in return, given that her husband loves the girl, the betrayed wife imposes on herself the obligation to love her equally and to arrange for the husband and the girl to be as comfortable in that bare room as they would be if they were in the family home. "Without my husband knowing," explains the wife to the spinner, "I will send you a large basin so that you can wash his feet frequently, a pile of firewood to keep him warm, a good bed, a feather quilt, sheets, and covers of the kind he is used to, bonnets for nighttime, cushions, stockings, and chemises. These I will send you clean, and you can

send them back to me for washing." The "householder of Paris" sees this as a useful example for his young wife of forbearance, wisdom, and charity—the story ends when the errant husband predictably repents[40]—but it also lets us slip into the bedrooms of the Middle Ages as the rich and the poor lie sleeping.

Other examples of the way the poor slept claim our attention as we come to the end of a day in a medieval city. The servants in Boccaccio's novella about King Agilulfo all sleep in the same room, sharing their beds: precisely this custom provides the mechanism of the plot, since the king has difficulty in finding, among so many heads, that of the treacherous servant (fig. 150).[41] The patients in the hospice-hospitals sleep together, with what reciprocal therapeutic effect we can well imagine

Figure 149. *The Charity of Saint Nicholas.* Gentile da Fabriano, detail from the predella of the Quaratesi polyptych, 1425. Rome, Pinacoteca Vaticana.

Figure 150. *Agilulfo in the Servants' Dormitory.* Pen and watercolor drawing, 1427, from Boccaccio, *Decameron* 3.2. Paris, Bibliothèque Nationale, MS It. 63, fol. 94v.

Figure 151. *A Hospital.* The sisters that assist represent the four cardinal virtues, prudence, temperance, justice, and fortitude. Miniature, fifteenth century, from the *Livre de la vie active des religieuses de l'Hôtel-Dieu.* Paris, Musée de l'Assistance Publique.

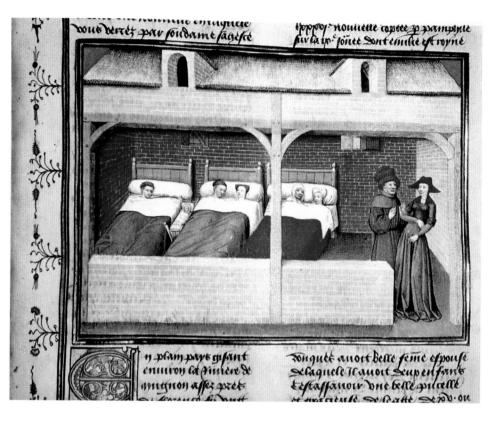

(fig. 151). Travelers sleep together when staying at inns; once again, a novella of Boc-caccio is based on the constant changing of beds during the night, for sharing the same room are the innkeeper's entire family and two guests who have arrived, one of whom burns with love for the daughter of that very innkeeper (fig. 152).

All sleep, and dream their dreams, until "at the crow of the cock, hope returns" (fig. 153).[42]

Figure 152. *A Room in an Inn.* Miniature, fifteenth century, from Boccaccio, *Decameron* 9.6. Paris, Bibliothèque de l'Arsenal, MS 5070, fol. 337r.

Figure 153. "At the crow of the cock, hope returns." Capital, eighth column on the left. Thirteenth century. Todi, Duomo.

Abbreviations

AA. SS. *Acta Sanctorum (Antwerp: Societé des Bollandistes, 1643—1940)*

MGH *Monumenta Germaniae Historica (Hannover and Leipzig, 1826—)*

PL *Patrologia Latina, ed. Jacques-Paul Migne (Paris, 1878—1890)*

RIS *Rerum Italicarum Scriptores, ed. L. A. Muratori (Milan: Ex Typographia Societatis Palatinae, 1723—51)*

Notes

Introduction

1. Lewis Mumford, *The City in History: Its Origins, Its Transformations, and Its Prospects* (New York: Harcourt, Brace, and World, 1961), ch. 10, p. 304.

2. Mumford, *City in History*, ch. 10, p. 309.

3. The word *patari*, meaning "rag dealers" or "old clothes dealers," comes from *patta* (probably derived from the Lombardic *paita*, "garment"), the word used by tailors to mean the flap that covers a pocket or the strip of fabric that covers a row of buttons.

4. Marc Bloch, *La société féudale* (1939; Paris: Albin Michel, 1968), pp. 117–118.

5. Helmholdi presbyteri Bozoviensis, *Cronica Slavorum* 1.55 (*MGH, Scriptores rerum Germanicarum*, ed. M. Lappenberg and B. Schmeidler [Hannover and Leipzig: Hahn 1909]): "Bella enim et tempestates, pestilentias et cetera humano generi inimica demonum ministerio fieri quis nesciat?"

6. Gregorii Turonensis, *De Gloria Martyrum* 1.28, cited in Arsenio Frugoni, *Il giubileo di Bonifacio VIII*, ed. Amedeo de Vincentiis (Bari: Laterza, 1999), p. 90.

7. This is a hymn of the twelfth or thirteenth century (it has been attributed to the Franciscan Tommaso da Celano), originally sung as part of the sequence for the first Sunday of Advent and later in the mass for the dead.

8. *Le mesnagier de Paris*, ed. G. E. Brereton, with facing translation in modern French (Paris: Le Livre de Poche, 1994), 1.7.3, pp. 298–299. This is a book of advice on domestic economy, combining kitchen recipes and religious and moral precepts, written around 1393 by a rich, elderly bourgeois of Paris for his young wife.

9. *Le mesnagier de Paris*, 2.5.334, pp. 788–789.

10. The Latin text is found in J. J. Baebler, *Beiträge zu einer Geschichte der lateinischen Grammatik im Mittelalter* (Halle a. S.: Buchhandlung des Waisenhauses, 1885), pp. 189–195. My thanks to Carla Frova for her bibliographic help in identifying this source.

11. Ekkeharti *Casus Sancti Galli*, ch. 67, in *St. Gallische Geschichtsquellen*, ed. G. Meyer

von Knonau; in *Mitteilungen zur Vaterländischen Geschichte,* Neue Folge, 5–6 Heft (15–16) (St. Gallen: Huber und Comp., 1877), p. 240.

12. Baebler, *Beiträge zu einer Geschichte der lateinischen Grammatik,* pp. 194–195.

13. G. Boccaccio, *Decameron,* ed. V. Branca, 2 vols. (Turin: Einaudi, 1993), from the "Introduction" to the First Day, p. 47 (in the English translation by Musa and Bondanella, p. 20.)

14. *Les cent nouvelles nouvelles,* ed. R. Dubuis (Lyon: Presses Universitaires de Lyon, 1991), nouvelle 19, "L'enfant de la neige," pp. 91–94. *Les cent nouvelles nouvelles* was written around 1460 at the court of Philip the Good, duke of Burgundy.

15. 1 Pet. 5: 8: "Be calm but vigilant, because your enemy the devil is prowling around like a roaring lion, looking for someone to eat."

16. *Le mesnagier de Paris,* 1.3.1, pp. 50–51.

CHAPTER ONE

1. V. Frandon, "Iconographie des saisons dans l'Occident médiéval," *Revue de la Bibliothèque Nationale* 50 (winter 1993): p. 2–8 and figure on 2.

2. Gen. 3:17.

3. See *Cantigas de Santa María: Edición facsímil del códice B.R. 20 de la Biblioteca Nazionale Centrale de Florencia, siglo XIII, El códice de Florencia de las Cantigas de Alfonso X el Sabio,* 2 vols. (Madrid: Edilán, 1989–1991), with the facsimile reproduction of the Florentine codex in vol. 1 and the text of the canticles in vol. 2. For the text of this canticle, see vol. 2, pp. 34–35.

4. Frandon, "Iconographie des saisons," p. 7. The representation of the Twelve Months, with each month identified by the particular labor of the peasant in that month, is almost always located in a church or other religious building. This is not a coincidence, because the representation of time through work, as a consequence of the sin of Adam, has an essentially religious connotation. It is rare for the Twelve Months to be depicted on a secular building.

CHAPTER TWO

1. Giovanni Villani, *Nuova cronica,* ed. G. Porta (Parma: U. Guanda, 1990–1991), 10.256, vol. 2, p. 428. At Siena in 1309 the order was given that the walls and facades of the houses built "within the city of Siena and its *borghi*" should be made of brick "in order that these houses endow the city with beauty." D. Balestracci and G. Piccinni, *Siena nel Trecento: Assetto urbano e strutture edilizie* (Siena: Clusf, 1977), p. 80. [TRANSLATOR'S NOTE: *braccio,* pl. *braccia,* literally "arm," was a measure of length that varied from town to town, but that was usually around 0.6 meter, or 2 feet.]

2. Dino Compagni, *Cronica delle cose occorrenti ne' tempi suoi,* ed. G. Bezzola (Milan: Rizzoli, 1995), 1.26, p. 107. This chronicle concludes in 1312.

3. The gates in the walls, which were closed at evening, were opened again very early every morning; an armed band of Sienese who set out to capture Figline in 1379 were counting on this: "Their plan was to arrive at Figline toward daylight, at the opening of the gate, which was opened in time for the workers," writes Marchionne di Coppo Stefani in the *Cronaca fiorentina* (Florentine chronicle) which he composed between 1378 and 1385 (*RIS* 30.1, rubric 824, p. 349; and for the dates of composition, p. xxviii). But they found the gate of the city barred, contrary to their design. For Marchionne's account of their escape, see below, ch. 3, n. 22.

4. *De Universo,* book 14 (*PL* 111, col. 384), cited by W. Braunfels, *Mittelalterliche Stadtbaukunst in der Toskana* (Berlin: G. Mann, 1959), p. 46.

5. C. Frugoni, *A Distant City: Images of Urban Experience in the Medieval World,* translated by W. McCuaig (Princeton: Princeton University Press, 1991), pp. 128–129, originally published as *Una lontana città:*

Sentimenti e immagini nel Medioevo (Turin: Einaudi, 1983); this reference at p. 144.

6.   *Le Biccherne: Tavole dipinte delle magistrature senesi (secoli XIII–XVIII),* ed. L. Borgia, E. Carli et al., 2d ed. (Rome: 1984), p. 182 and the figure at p. 183. A biccherna panel (*tavoletta di biccherna*) is a small painted panel used as the decorative cover of one of the registers of the treasury of the commune of Siena.

7.   These colors coincide with those of the three main quarters of Siena: vermilion for Città; green for San Martino; white for Camollia. Paolo di Tommaso Montauri, *Cronaca senese conosciuta sotto il nome di Paolo di Tommaso Montauri, RIS* 15.6, fasc. 8, pp. 179–252, pp. 689–835, p. 741.

8.   "If (as the philosophers maintain) the city is like some large house, and the house is in turn like some small city . . ." wrote Leon Battista Alberti in the Renaissance. *De re aedificatoria* 1.9, cited in Frugoni, *A Distant City,* p. 4, n. 4; English translation, Leon Battista Alberti, *On the Art of Building in Ten Books,* translated by Joseph Rykwert, Neil Leach, and Robert Tavernor (Cambridge, Mass., and London: MIT Press, 1988), p. 23.

9.   Giordano da Pisa, *Prediche recitate in Firenze dal 1303 al 1306 ed ora per la prima volta pubblicate,* ed. C. Moreni (Florence: Magheri, 1831), vol. 1, p. 96.

10.   *El códice de Florencia de las Cantigas de Alfonso X el Sabio,* vol. 1, fol. 2 (for the reproduction), and vol. 2, pp. 22–23 (for the text).

11.   L Zdekauer, *La vita pubblica dei senesi nel Dugento* (Siena: L. Lazzeri, 1897), p. 101. Villani registers, for the year 1310, the precautions taken at Florence against the dreaded arrival of the emperor, Henry VII: new moats were dug and sections of the wall restored, "inasmuch as the city was wide open, the old walls having been largely torn down and sold to abutting neighbors so as to enlarge the old city and comprise the *borghi* and the new accretion." *Nuova cronica,* 10.10, vol. 2, p. 219. At Perugia in 1266 and again in 1378 there were violent uprisings because the *borghi* felt discriminated against on account of the fact that at night the gates of the old city were closed. U. Nicolini, "Mura della città e mura dei borghi: La coscienza urbanistica di Perugia medievale," in Nicolini, *Scritti di storia* (Naples: Edizioni Scientifiche Italiane, 1993), pp. 138–157, esp. pp. 146–147.

12.   "Si Deus non custodierit civitatem meam, frustra vigilat qui custodiat eam" (an adaptation of the text of Psalm 126:1 in the Vulgate; Psalm 127:1 in other versions. Braunfels, *Mittelalterliche Stadtbaukunst,* p. 53, n. 118.

13.   Braunfels, *Mittelalterliche Stadtbaukunst,* p. 84.

14.   *Statutes of Verona,* rubric n. 209; W. Braunfels, *Mittelalterliche Stadtbaukunst,* p. 83 and 83–85 for many other interesting examples.

15.   "Frammenti di statuti di Città di Castello 1261–1273," edited by G. Magherini-Graziani, in *Bollettino di Storia Patria per l'Umbria* 15 (1909): 3–107, here at 26; cited by Marco Grondona, *Le stazioni di ieri: Prolegomeni ad una guida dell'Umbria* (Spoleto: Centro Italiano di Studi sull'Alto Medioevo, 1991), p. 50 (with many other examples), and n. 112.

16.   A. Messini and F. Baldaccini, eds., *Statuta Communis Fulginei,* Fonti per la storia dell'Umbria, no. 6, 2 vols. (Perugia: Deputazione di Storia Patria per l'Umbria, 1969;), vol. 1, p. 187, rubric 94.

17.   Cited in A. Vauchez, *La sainteté en Occident aux derniers siècles du Moyen Age* (Rome: École française de Rome, 1981), p. 526, n. 21.

18.   There is even an arrow that, when discharged in the direction of the saint, turns around and blinds the pagan king who is persecuting him, until the protracted martyrdom ends with a decapitation.

19.   The legend of Saint Christopher became much more popular than his *passio* because it was diffused in a book widely copied and read, the *Legenda aurea* of the Dominican Iacopo da Varagine (da Varazze; in Latin, Jacobus a Voragine), *Legenda aurea,* ed. Th. Graesse (Osnabrück: Zeller, 1969;

a photoreprint of the 1890 edition), ch. C (95), "De Sancto Christophoro," pp. 430–434.

20. *AA. SS.,* Julii, VI (Antwerp: J. du Moulin, 1729), "De s. Christophoro martyre Jacobus," pp. 125–149, esp. p. 135 and n. 57.

21. The baby Jesus (on the shoulders of Saint Christopher) holds the world on the tip of his finger as though it were a top: a happy observation of the sort of gesture babies make. See C. Brandi, ed., *Palazzo Pubblico di Siena: Vicende costruttive e decorazione* (Siena: Monte dei Paschi di Siena, 1983), p. 232 and fig. 300. The height comes close to rivaling the stupendous eight-meter-tall portrait of Saint Christopher at Santa Nicola in Treviso, or the one in the Cathedral of Spilimbergo, near Pordenone; portraits on this scale are meant to be visible from a distance. G. Milanesi, *Documenti per la storia dell'arte senese* (Siena: Porri, 1856), vol. 2, p. 192; and D. Rigaux, "Usages apotropaïques de la fresque dans l'Italie du Nord au XIVe siècle," in *Nicée II, 787–1987: Douze siècles d'images religieuses,* ed. F. Boesflug and N. Lossky (Paris: Éditions du Cerf, 1987), pp. 317–331, esp. p. 323.

22. *Palazzo Pubblico di Siena,* p. 417.

23. *Palazzo Pubblico di Siena,* p. 342, n. 215.

24. *Palazzo Pubblico di Siena,* p. 193.

25. *Palazzo Pubblico di Siena,* p. 420.

26. "Thadeus Bartoli de Senis pinxit istam cappellam mccccvii cum figura sancti Christophori et cum istis aliis figuris." *Palazzo Pubblico di Siena,* p. 241. The chapel was painted in 1407, the embrasure leading to it starting in January 1408.

27. L. Berti, ed., *Il museo di Palazzo Davanzati a Firenze* (Milan: Electa, n.d.), fig. 2.

28. Rigaux, "Usages apotropaïques de la fresque," p. 324.

29. See F. Flores d'Arcais, "Giovanni da Bologna," in *Enciclopedia dell'Arte medioevale* (Rome: Treccani, 1995), vol. 6, pp. 715–16 and the fig. at p. 715. The panel is located at the Museo Civico of Padua.

30. "Christophorum videas, postea tutus eas"; or "Christophore sancte, virtutes tuae sunt tantae: / qui te mane videt nocturno tempore ridet"; or again: "Christophori sancti speciem quicumque tuetur / ista nempe die non morte mala morietur." On this topic, see Rigaux, "Usages apotropaïques de la fresque," p. 324.

31. G. Kaftal, *Iconography of the Saints in Tuscan Painting* (Florence: Sansoni, 1952), p. 268, fig. 309.

32. Boccaccio, *Decameron* 2.2 (trans. Musa and Bondanella, pp. 67–68).

33. Boccaccio, *Decameron* 2.2 (trans. Musa and Bondanella, pp. 68–69).

34. Numerous bands of robbers, domineering and killing, propel the tale of Pietro Boccamazza and his beloved in novella 5.3 of the *Decameron.* Pietro, separated from Agnolella because of the sudden arrival of such a band, wanders in the forest, "and while he dared not go back, he had no idea of where he would end up by going ahead; and then also he was afraid both for himself and for the girl of the wild beasts that lurked in the forests, and he kept imagining the girl being torn apart by a bear or a wolf." Boccaccio, *Decameron* 5.3 (trans. Musa and Bondanella, p. 331).

35. The regime of the Nine at Siena lasted from 1287 to 1355.

36. Cf. F. Santi, *Gonfaloni umbri del Rinascimento* (Perugia: Editrice Volumnia, 1976), p. 16 and fig. 2.

37. From the records of the Sienese magistracy dedicated to roads and transportation that tried to maintain the practicability of the roadways and bridges and the security of wayfarers: "The thoroughfares of the city of Siena are paved; and there are some streets that debouch and open into the thoroughfares that are not paved, on account of which the thoroughfares are befouled, because the filth and mud from those streets flow into the thoroughfares." Balestracci and Piccinni, *Siena nel Trecento,* p. 41.

38. The use of bricks for paving was an innovation of the thirteenth century; before that the streets of Siena were paved with flagstones, in the Roman manner. Balestracci and Piccinni, *Siena nel*

Trecento, p. 57, cite a contemporary source: "In this year [1241] they began to make the paving stones out of brick, something that had never been done before." The statute of the road magistracy for 1290, under rubric 8, orders that the road inside and outside Porta San Giorgio, which was paved with stone ("quae via est de lapidibus") should be covered with brick, and the former flint paving stones removed ("et quod silex lapidum ibi factus destruatur"). Zdekauer, *La vita pubblica dei Senesi,* p. 104.

39. "In civitate et extra civitatem Senarum per totum comitatum" (within the city of Siena, and throughout the whole surrounding district). T. Szabó, "La rete stradale del contado di Siena: Legislazione statutaria e amministrazione comunale del Duecento," in *Mélanges de l'École française de Rome* 87 (1975): 141–186, here at 159.

40. Ambrogio Lorenzetti, in a depiction of the martyrdom of three Franciscans at what is today Bombay ("a huge and egregiously executed narrative," wrote Lorenzo Ghiberti), was the first to represent a storm pictorially: "we see the onset of a tremendous storm; the sky darkens, hail falls, there are thunderbolts, and we seem to hear them rumble . . . for a painting, it seems to me that this storm has been rendered in a marvelous fashion." Lorenzo Ghiberti, *I Commentari,* ed. Ottavio Morisani (Naples: Ricciardi, 1947), II, 2, p. 37. During the work to restructure the ex-cloister of San Francesco at Siena a few fragments of this fresco came to light, and the largest of them belongs to this storm scene. Piero Torrito, ed., *Mostra di opere d'arte restaurate nelle province di Siena e Grosseto* (Genoa: Sagep, 1979), pp. 58–60 and fig. 47.

41. [Giordano da Pisa], *Prediche sulla Genesi recitate in Firenze nel 1304 dal beato fra Giordano da Rivalto,* ed. D. Moreni (Florence: Magheri, 1830), sermon 35, pp. 196–197. In the preceding sermon, no. 34, he had on the other hand denied (p. 192) the widespread belief that when the rebel angels were precipitated into hell, rain and hailstorms poured down uninterruptedly for nine days.

42. *Brevia* (singular *breve;* English "brief") in this context means little wrappings of fabric containing a relic or a formulaic prayer, worn around the neck for devotion.

43. Anonymus Ticinensis (Opicino de Canistris), *Liber de laudibus civitatis Ticinensis, RIS* 11,1, pp. 1–52, p. 32, para. 35 and ff.

44. The episode of the angel and the epigraph placed on the tomb of Agatha, but without any explanation, is reported by Iacopo da Varazze in chapter 39 of the *Legenda aurea,* p. 173, which is dedicated to her.

45. C. Grondona, *Todi: Storica ed artistica,* with additions by M. Grondona (Todi: Pro Todi Editrice, 1993), p. 76 with ample commentary, fig. 45, and p. 85.

46. The bell bears the following inscription in leonine verses: "Anno Domini 1239. Papae Gregorii tempore noni, Cesaris ac potentissimi Friderici. O Francise pie / Fratris studio sed Helie, Christus / regnat, Christus vincit, Christus imperat. Mentem sanctam, spontaneam, honorem Deo et patriae liberationem. /Cum fit campana que dicitur Italiana, Bartholomaeus fecit cum Lotaringio filius eius. /Ave Maria, gratia plena, Dominus tecum, benedicta tu / in mulieribus et benedictus fructus ventris tui." G. Zaccaria, "Diario storico della Basilica e Sacro Convento di S. Francesco in Assisi (1220–1927)," in *Miscellanea Francescana* 63 (1963): 75–120, 290–361, 495–536; see 83, no. 21. In medieval Latin and Romance poetry, leonine verses (perhaps from the name of a poet of the twelfth century, Leonius) was the term for verses in which the first hemistich chimes, by rhyme or assonance, with the second, or the same assonance or rhyme is used repeatedly.

47. In the *Memoriale degli Unti* (Pietruccio di Giacomo degli Unti), which covers the period 1424–1440 (*RIS* 26, 2, p. 35, n. 2), the inscription on the bell at Foligno is given: "Christus vincit. Christus regnat. Christus imperat. Hoc opus factum fuit tempore Domini Raynaldi de Trincis electi Fulginensis, MCCCCXXXVIII. Mentem sanctam, spontaneam, honorem Deo et patriae liberationem."

48. Gulielmi Durandi, *Rationale divinorum officiorum* (Venice: apud Cominum de Tridino, 1572), 1.4, "De campanis," fol. 13v.

49. Durandi, *Rationale divinorum officiorum,* fol. 14.

CHAPTER THREE

1. Franco Sacchetti, *Il Trecentonovelle,* ed. E. Faccioli (Turin: Einaudi, 1970), novella 115, pp. 299–300.

2. *Palazzo Davanzati,* ed. M. F. Todorow (Florence: Becocci, 1979), fig. no. 21, and p. 49; *Il museo di Palazzo Davanzati,* tav. XIV.

3. The codex, amply illuminated (Paris, Bibl. Nat. 1463), was probably copied in Liguria by the Italian writer Rustichello da Pisa, who used French to retell the tales of King Arthur and the knights of the Round Table: *Il Romanzo arturiano di Rustichello da Pisa,* ed. F. Cini (Pisa: Cassa di Risparmio di Pisa, 1994). The miniature with the duel of Lancelot is at fol. 60v.

4. The throat armor was called a *gorgiera;* the armor worn on the arm was called a *bracciaiuola.*

5. Sacchetti, *Il Trecentonovelle,* novella 115, p. 302. The gesture of the donkey driver recalls that of Vanni Fucci in Dante *Inferno* 25, 1–3.

6. When Florence was briefly the capital of the new Kingdom of Italy in the nineteenth century, building renewal projects were carried out that destroyed, among other things, an entire cluster of fourteenth-century houses, including the house of the Teri, which stood in the quarter of the Mercato Vecchio. Fragments of the fresco of Isolde, which were kept until 1936 in the storage area of the Museum of San Marco in Florence, are today unlocatable. C. Frugoni, "Le decorazioni murali come testimonianza di uno 'status symbol,'" in *Un palazzo, una città: Il palazzo Lanfranchi* (Pisa: Pacini, 1980), pp. 141–145, esp. p. 144.

7. Perhaps by the minstrel Antonio Pucci (1310–1390). *Il museo di Palazzo Davanzati,* pp. 14ff., and figs. 29, 30, 35, and 36.

8. Juan Ruiz, *The Book of Good Love,* trans. Elizabeth Drayson Macdonald (London: J. M. Dent, 1999), lines 723a–c. Little is known of this author, who was the archpriest of Hita in Spain, and the few dates of his life are derivable only from his work, which was composed between 1330 and 1343.

9. Ruiz, *Book of Good Love,* line 957d (the shepherd girl); stanzas 1003–1004 (the mountain girl); lines 171b–c (the fine lady).

10. That is, she was reciting prayers following the canonical hours. *Le mesnagier de Paris,* 1.4.15, pp. 144–145.

11. Sacchetti, *Il Trecentonovelle,* novella 84, pp. 219–220.

12. Sacchetti, *Il Trecentonovelle,* novella 84, p. 221.

13. The tale finishes well for the lover, who is discovered but still manages to escape.

14. According to Sacchetti, the woman used to stay "up on the roofs all day; some curling their hair, some making it smooth, some making it lighter in color; so that they often die of catarrh." Sacchetti, *Il Trecentonovelle,* novella 178, p. 524.

15. At Siena, from 1262 on, the dimensions of these counters (*banchi*) were regulated by the city council. Balestracci and Piccinni, *Siena nel Trecento,* p. 46.

16. Those who repair shoes are still called *calzolai* today. This name derives from the medieval custom of sewing a sole directly onto the bottom of the tight stockings or leggings (*calze*) worn by men, so that their footwear and their legwear formed one piece. On top of these soled tights, they might also cover their feet with shoes or clogs.

17. *L'Umbria: Manuali per il territorio; Spoleto,* ed. L. Gentili, L. Giacché, B. Ragni, and B. Toscano (Rome: Edindustria, 1978), third itinerary, figures on pp. 260–261: Via del Palazzo dei Duchi, the shops (*botteghe*) of the "Stradetta."

18. Boccaccio, *Decameron* 6.2 (trans. Musa and Bondanella, pp. 384–386).

19. Sacchetti, *Il Trecentonovelle,* novella 76, pp. 194–196.

20. Sacchetti, *Il Trecentonovelle,* novella 151, pp. 409–410.

21. Marchionne di Coppo Stefani, *Cronaca fiorentina,* rubric 967, p. 431.

22. Marchionne di Coppo Stefani, *Cronaca fiorentina,* rubric 824, p. 349.

23. Villani, *Nuova cronica,* 9.99, vol. 2, p. 177.

24. "Lo guardiano che stava nella terra cominciò a chiamare le guardie; udendo il romore . . ." The semicolon after *guardie* is my punctuation. Sacchetti's editor, Faccioli, inserted a comma at this point, which seems to me to make the sentence arduous.

25. Sacchetti, *Il Trecentonovelle,* novella 132, pp. 341–343.

26. Villani, *Nuova cronica,* 10.158, vol. 2, p. 356.

27. "Frammenti di statuti di Città di Castello, 1261–1273," ed. Magherini-Graziani, p. 42; the passage quoted comes from the statute of 1261.

28. *Liber statutorum Civitatis Castelli* (Città di Castello: Antonio Mazzocchi and Nicola and Bartolomeo Gucci, 1538), fols. 51r and 57r.

29. *Liber statutorum Civitatis Castelli,* fol. 57v. In December 1344 at Florence the bell of the people that rang to summon the council was moved from the crenels of the Palazzo dei Priori (known today as Palazzo Vecchio or Palazzo della Signoria) to a place higher up on the tower so that it could be heard better in the part of the city across the Arno River. In its place was put "the bell that came from the castle of Vernia, and it was ordered to be rung only when a fire started in the city at night, so that at the sound of it the master masons, and those whose job is fighting fires, would come quickly." Villani, *Nuova cronica,* 13.36, vol. 3, p. 382.

30. Two or three cases, a mattress and a pillow, a basin full of plates scattered about—this short list of things that were saved actually amounts to an indication that little or nothing was saved from the fire.

31. Durandus, *Rationale divinorum officiorum,* 1.4, fol. 14v.

32. It is the "puteus abyssi," "the pit of the abyss," of Revelations 9:2.

33. The sculptures are dated to the last quarter of the twelfth century by J. Esch, *La chiesa di San Pietro a Spoleto* (Florence: Olschki, 1981), pp. 100–101, and figs. 56–57.

34. *Cronaca senese* by Donato di Neri and his son Neri, *RIS,* 15, 6, p. 591. This chronicle goes from 1352 to 1381.

35. *Statuti del castello di Corciano,* ed. G. Scentoni (Perugia: Cooperativa della Regione dell'Umbria, 1982), rubric 29, p. 43.

36. Sacchetti, *Il Trecentonovelle,* novella 112, pp. 293–294.

37. L. Fiumi, *Gli statuti di Chianciano dell'anno 1287* (Orvieto, 1874), rubric 277, p. 133, and rubric 17, p. 17.

38. Zdekauer, *La vita pubblica dei Senesi nel Dugento,* p. 137.

39. An influential work on this subject is J. Le Goff, *Pour un autre Moyen Age: Temps, travail et culture en Occident; 18 essais* (Paris: Gallimard, 1977); Italian translation, *Tempo della Chiesa e tempo del mercante* (Turin: Einaudi, 1977); English translation, *Time, Work, and Culture in the Middle Ages,* trans. Arthur Goldhammer (Chicago: University of Chicago Press, 1980).

40. C. Frugoni, "Das Schachspiel in der Welt des Jacobus de Cessolis," in *Das Schachbuch des Jacobus de Cessolis, Codex Palatinus Latinus 961* (Stuttgart: Belser, 1988), pp. 35–75, esp. pp. 52ff. For the text of Jacobus de Cessolis, *Liber de moribus hominum ac officiis nobilium super ludo scaccorum,* it is still necessary to rely on the old edition of E. Köpke (Brandenburg: 1879; *Mitteilungen aus den Handschriften der Ritterakademie*

zu Brandenburg, Heft I I, appendix to XXIII Jahrbericht, Programm nr. 59); I have never located a copy in Italy, but only at Wolfenbüttel. Cf. pp. 28 and 30.

41. See p. 90.

42. Text published in appendix 6 of Zdekauer, *La vita pubblica dei Senesi nel Dugento,* pp. 188–189.

43. Biblioteca comunale di Città di Castello, *Riformanze,* vol. 34, fol. 31v, for 13 June 1407: "Quod de cetero prior hospitalis sancti Antonii de Civitate Castelli possit licite et libere, sine pena retinere per civitatem extra domos hic inde eundo per civitatem duos porcos nutriendos pro pauperibus domini nostri Jehsu Cristi." Archivio di Stato di Gubbio, Fondo Comunale, *Riformanze,* vol. 14, fol. 140r, for 23 December 1391: "Quod rector ecclesiae S. Antonii de Eugubio possit et sibi liceat mictere et retinere . . . unum porcellum" [and may] "ipsos porcellos in dictis castris retinendos signare in spatula dextra signo montis et Thau in auricula sinistra incisa, et cum campanella adposita ad auriculam dextram impune." The Anonymus Ticinensis (Opicino de Canistris, that is), *Liber de laudibus,* p. 36, records that at Pavia the friars of sant'Antonio received not only money and alms of various sorts, but also "porcos multos nutritos in publico." As for the letter *tau* (the letter *T* in the Greek and Hebraic alphabets), with which Saint Anthony's swine in Gubbio were meant to be branded on the left ear, it represents the form of the typical hermit's staff or sick person's crutch. See *Porci e porcari nel Medioevo, paesaggio, economia, alimentazione,* ed. M. Baruzzi and M. Montanari (Bologna: Clueb, 1981), p. 64.

44. *Porci e porcari nel Medioevo,* p. 64.

45. Sacchetti, *Il Trecentonovelle,* novella 75, p. 193.

46. Sacchetti, *Il Trecentonovelle,* novella 110, pp. 287–290.

47. Boccaccio *Decameron,* introduction to day 1 (trans. Musa and Bondanella, p. 7).

48. Marchionne di Coppo Stefani, *Cronaca fiorentina,* rubric 634, p. 231.

49. When the elderly Parisian husband whom we have met counsels his young wife to examine her conscience, and comes to the sin of pride, he suggests that she make the following acknowledgment: "I have given nothing to the poor in the name of God. On the contrary, I was filled with contempt and disdain toward them. Since they all seemed to me repugnant, fetid, and stinking, I did not allow them to approach and hastened away to avoid seeing them." *Le mesnagier de Paris,* 1.3, 39, pp. 76–77.

50. C. Frugoni, "Altri luoghi, cercando il paradiso (il ciclo di Buffalmacco nel Camposanto di Pisa e la committenza domenicana)," in *Annali della Scuola Normale Superiore di Pisa,* series 3, vol. 18, no. 4 (1988, but published in 1990): p. 1557–1643, esp. p. 1577 and 1577ff.

51. *El códice de Florencia,* vol. 1, p. 88 and vol. 2, fol. 88r.

52. [Giordano da Pisa], *Prediche inedite del B. Giordano da Rivalto dell'ordine de' Predicatori recitate in Firenze dal 1302 al 1305,* ed. E. Narducci (Bologna: G. Romagnoli, 1867), sermon 10, p. 53.

53. [Giordano da Pisa], *Prediche del B. Giordano da Rivalto dell'ordine de' Predicatori (del 1304, dell'Avvento e della Quaresima),* ed. M. D. Manni (Florence: G. Viviani, 1739), sermon 33, p. 146.

54. The documents cited here (in an English translation) are published in P. Riché and D. Alexandre-Bidon, *L'enfance au Moyen Âge* (Paris: Seuil, 1994), p. 177. In this book I encountered the figures that in my book are numbered 66, 89–91, 94–95, 101, 103, 105–110, 114–115, 117, 120–121.

55. The fresco is preserved in a fragmentary state. See *Il museo del Bigallo a Firenze,* ed. H. Kiel (Milan: Electa, 1977), p. 5, pp. 120–121, and figs. 42–48.

56. The Palazzo Pubblico, that is, on the Piazza del Campo, where the Nine had their offices.

57. G. Pinto, *Il libro del Biadaiolo: Carestie e annona a Firenze dalla metà del '200 al 1348* (Florence: Olschki, 1978), p. 320 (fol. 56v). In one of Sacchetti's novellas, set in Florence, a horse created a disturbance among the stalls of the clothsellers at Calimala, then among the grain merchants and their barrels at Orsanmichele; and amid the general confusion it was the blind who got the worst of it: "And some

of the blind who always cluster in large numbers in the said place at the Pilaster [near Orsanmichele], hearing the noise and being pushed and trampled, and not knowing the cause of the uproar, began swinging their staffs and dealing blows to others left and right. Most of those who were struck rounded on them, not knowing that they were blind. Others, who did know that they were blind, verbally attacked those who were attacking them; and then the second group attacked the third. And so on all sides everyone started hitting everyone else, with scuffles breaking out all over the place." Sacchetti, *Il Trecentonovelle,* novella 159, pp. 448–449. Although the source here is an excerpt from a novella and not a chronicle, it is clear that the author, writing for a contemporary audience, must have been describing utterly verisimilar situations.

58. Pinto, *Il libro del Biadaiolo,* p. 322, fol. 59r.

59. *Testamentum,* in *Sancti Patris Francisci Assisiensis Opuscula,* ed. K. Esser (Grottaferrata [Rome]: Coll. S. Bonaventurae, 1978), pp. 307–317, here at pp. 307–308.

60. Sacchetti, *Il Trecentonovelle,* novella 207, p. 632.

61. *Liber statutorum Civitatis Castelli,* fol. 47r, the penalty for a thief: "Fustigetur per Civitatem Castelli et ducatur ad petronem communis et ibidem cum ferro callido in guancea coquatur, et ligetur et moretur ibi saltem duabus horis." In the same city of Città di Castello, in 1399, a very similar penalty was imposed, in absentia, on a certain Musetto, a Jew of Ancona, for theft; Biblioteca comunale di Città di Castello, *Riformanze,* vol. 9, part 2, fol 90r.

62. *Liber statutorum Civitatis Castelli,* fol. 41v, the penalty for a blasphemer: "Fustigetur per Civitatem Castelli a porta Sanctae Mariae Maioris usque ad portam Sancti Juliani . . . cum tenaglis in lingua."

63. *Liber statutorum Civitatis Castelli,* fol. 46v, the penalty for a murderer: "Traginetur per Civitatem ad caudam equi, muli vel asini et suspendatur per gulam ita quod penitus moriatur."

64. At Città di Castello in 1397 charges were brought in absentia against "Casciolum Rici de Civitate Castelli et porta s. Marie, hominem proditorem, coniuratorem, tractatorem, sediciosum, turbatorem popularis et pacifici status civitatis prefate, sollicitatorem, concitatorem sedicionum et tumultus"; should he be captured, "tanquam proditor ligetur ad caudam aselli et sic ligatus trahatur et trahi debeat per loca publica et consueta dicte Civitatis Castelli usque ad locum iustitie consuetum, ibique plantetur et plantari debeat cum capite deorsum et tantum tempore sic plantatus stare debeat quousque moriatur et penitus eius anima a corpo separetur." Biblioteca comunale di Città di Castello, *Riformanze,* vol. 9, part 2, fols. 39r, 42v.

65. Sacchetti, *Il Trecentonovelle,* novella 182, p. 528.

66. Zdekauer, *La vita pubblica dei Senesi nel Dugento,* pp. 98–99. The minutes of the council meeting are printed in appendix 4, pp. 184–186. For once, the voice of moderation finally prevailed.

67. Paolo di Tommaso Montauri, *Cronaca senese,* p. 723, cited in Balestracci and Piccinni, *Siena nel Trecento,* p. 165.

68. "Justicia facta de Thebaldo capitaneo Brixie" (Justice done to Thebaldus, captain of Brescia) is written under the drawing. *Il viaggio di Enrico VII in Italia,* ed. M. Tosti-Croce (Città di Castello: Ministero per i Beni culturali- Edimond, 1993), fig. 13. The manuscript, commissioned by the brother of Henry VII, Archbishop Baldwin of Trier, must have been executed between 1340 and circa 1350. V. Kessel, however, in "Il manoscritto del 'viaggio a Roma,'" pp. 13–28 in the same volume, reviews the dates proposed by previous scholars and prefers a date circa 1330 (p. 21), but adduces no decisive arguments.

69. C. Frugoni, "Altri luoghi," p. 1570.

70. J. Baschet, *Les justices de l'au-delà: Les représentation de l'Enfer en France et en Italie (XII–XV siècle)* (Rome and Paris: École française de Rome, 1993), pp. 293, 293ff.

71. Bernardino da Siena, *Le prediche volgari,* ed. C. Cannarozzi (Pistoia: Pacinotti, 1934), vol. 1, p. 244; the prophecies attributed to the British magician Merlin were widely known in the Middle

Ages; see p. 253. San Bernardino deals with the same topic, in almost the same words, in his Lenten cycle of 1425: Bernardino da Siena, *Le prediche volgari,* vol. 4 (Florence: Libreria Editrice Fiorentina, 1940), p. 226. On this detail of Orcagna's fresco, see C. Frugoni, "La coppia infernale di Andrea Orcagna in Santa Croce a Firenze: Proposta per una possibile fonte della novella di Nastagio degli Onesti," in *Studi sul Boccaccio* 28 (2000): 99–104.

72.   G. Ortalli, ". . . *Pingatur in Palatio* . . .": *La pittura infamante nei secoli XII–XVI* (Rome: Jouvence, 1979), idem, "La rappresentazione politica e i nuovi confini dell'immagine nel secolo XIII," in *L'image: Fonctions et usages des images dans l'Occident médiéval* (Paris: Le Léopard d'or, 1996), pp. 251–275.

73.   Not all friars were as deft at adapting their sermons to the expectations and the consensus of their audience as San Bernardino was. Sacchetti portrays the hesitant inception of a young friar of the Augustinian hermits, who preached in the evening at Santa Reparata in Florence during Lent. His audience at that hour, "when the shops were closed," consisted of "all the poor wool workers" and "youths and girls and servants." The friar emphasized the sin of usury and the damnation it entails until in the darkness of the church a voice burst out ("and everyone looked around as if bewildered to see where this voice came from, since it was so dark"): "I want you to know that you are wasting your breath, because everyone you see here at this sermon takes loans, they don't make them, because they don't have the wherewithal, I least of all. So if you know how to give us some relief in the matter of our debts, and of what we have to pay to others, please do. If not, then I and the rest that are here will dispense with coming to your sermons." Sacchetti, *Il Trecentonovelle,* novella 100, pp. 263–264.

74.   "San Bernardino of Siena preaches in Spello for all of Lent, he divides the men from the women in church with a cloth; he institutes the company of the Name of Jesus, and the altar piece he carried in his hand with the name of Jesus he leaves to the convent of Sant'Andrea, of this place." M. Faloci Pulignani, "Le Cronache di Spello degli Olorini," in *Bollettino della Deputazione di Storia Patria dell'Umbria* 23 (1918): pp. 239–298, here at p. 283 for the sermon of 1442. This chronicle was begun by Giovanni Olorini, who died in 1388, and was continued by other members of his family.

75.   Bernardino da Siena, *Le prediche volgari,* vol. 1, p. 245.

76.   "Itaque cum esset juvenis et laicus in domo patris sui, et sanctitatis, ut dictum est, amator, forte quadam die audivit mimum cantando referentem vitam et conversionem sancti Theobaldi et asperitatem vitam eius." E. Faral, *Les Jongleurs en France au Moyen Âge* (1910; 2d. ed., Paris: H. Champion, 1971), app. 3, n. 69b, from the *Vita sancti Ayberti* (d. 1140), *AA. SS.,* Aprilis (Antwerp: 1675), t. 1, p. 674, 5. For many other examples, see C. Frugoni, "La rappresentazione dei giullari nelle chiese fino al XII sec.," in *Il Contributo dei giullari alla drammaturgia italiana delle origini: Atti del II Convegno di Studio, Viterbo, 17–19 giugno '77* (Rome: Bulzoni, 1978), pp. 113–134, at pp. 123–24.

77.   Often it is the commune that undertakes to pay the cost of the entertainment. From the *Riformanze* in the Biblioteca comunale di Città di Castello, vol. 36, fol. 129r, for 23 August 1411: "Quod . . . camerarius comunis de ipsius comunis pecunia det et solvat istis tubatoribus, menestreriis et ioculatoribus qui venerunt et honoraverunt festum sanctorum Floridi et Amantii istas pecunias."

78.   Sacchetti, *Il Trecentonovelle,* novella 69, pp. 175–176.

79.   According to Sacchetti, gaming with dice, or "zara," ought to be suppressed, because it amounts to "blaspheming God, consuming riches, conjoining pride and anger, seeking opportunities to steal and rob because of avarice." He even expresses approval of a crime committed by a man who, having lost everything to dice, killed the artisan who had made them. Sacchetti, *Il Trecentonovelle,* novella 122, pp. 319–320.

80.   While Lancelot, exhausted after a tourney, was resting, "there arrived a wretched individual, a herald of arms, in his shirt, who had left his tunic and his leggings at the tavern as a pledge, and came barefoot, with little protection against the wind." Chrétien de Troyes, *Lancillotto,* in idem, *Romanzi* (Florence: Sansoni, 1962), p. 334. [TRANSLATOR'S NOTE: The English version here is made from the

Italian one cited by C. Frugoni, not the Old French original, *Lancelot*]. Cecco Angiolieri (1260–1311 or 1313), however, exalts a life of dissipation, one requiring a lot of spending money, in his sonnet 87: "I like only three things / and I can't get enough of them: / that is, women, the tavern, and dice; / *these* make my heart light. / But I am forced to enjoy them so rarely, / since my purse has other plans for me." *Cecco As I Am and Was: The Poems of Cecco Angiolieri,* trans. Tracy Barrett (Boston: Branden, 1994), 105.

81. *El códice de Florencia,* vol. 1, pp. 38–39 and vol. 2, fol. 20r.

82. In Siena this would have been an offence, as the law stated that "no poltroon or ribald or gambler, or anyone else of bad repute may or should play at any game of dice and gambling within a distance of 60 braccia of any church in the city." Balestracci and Piccinni, *Siena nel Trecento,* p. 61.

83. A. Rizzi, *Ludus/ludere: Giocare in Italia alla fine del Medioevo* (Rome: Viella, 1995); G. Ortalli, ed., *Gioco e giustizia nell'Italia di Comune* (Treviso and Rome: Benetton-Viella, 1993).

84. A. Settia, "La 'battaglia': Un gioco violento fra permissività e interdizione," in Ortalli, *Gioco e giustizia,* pp. 121–132; and Rizzi, *Ludus/ludere,* esp. pp. 99–101, with ample bibliography.

85. I will not discuss ceremonial competitions (*palii*), warlike and peaceful (for the origin and significance of which readers are referred to the final chapter of Rizzi, *Ludus/ludere,* "'Pro bravio sive palio currendo': Un gioco promosso nell'Italia dei Comuni," pp. 171–204): they are too much tied, even the peaceful ones, to significant religious and political events in local memory to play a part in this ramble of mine through an average day in a distant city.

86. C. Frugoni, "La rappresentazione dei giullari," pp. 122–123.

87. C. Frugoni, "La rappresentazione dei giullari," p. 123; and the reproduction in *Enciclopedia Universale dell'Arte* (Venice: Istituto per la collaborazione culturale Venezia-Roma, 1964), s.v. "scenografia" by E. Povoledo, vol. 12, tav. 153.

88. Marchionne di Coppo Stefani, *Cronaca fiorentina,* rubric 777, p. 309.

89. The very detailed list of expenditures was compiled on 27 April 1291, five days after the death of Masino; for the exact figures, see Zdekauer, *La vita pubblica dei Senesi nel Dugento,* appendix 7, pp. 103–104.

90. C. Thomasset, "The Nature of Women," chapter 2 of *Silences of the Middle Ages,* ed. Christiane Klapisch-Zuber, vol. 2 of *A History of Women in the West,* ed. G. Duby and M. Perrot (Cambridge, Mass.: Belknap Press of Harvard University Press, 1992), pp. 43–69.

91. Vair (in Italian, *vaio;* from the Latin *varius,* "variegated in color") is the medieval name given to fur made from the coat of a Siberian squirrel (corresponding to the one known in Western Europe as *petit-gris*), which in winter is entirely gray except for its white chest. The fur has the appearance of a series of white shields on a gray background.

92. "... sempre portava una foggia altissima, con un becchetto corto da lato, e largo che vi serebbe entrato mezzo staio di grano, e con due batoli dinanzi che pareano due sugnacci di porco affumicati." Sacchetti, *Il Trecentonovelle,* novella 155, p. 429.

93. Sacchetti, *Il Trecentonovelle,* novella 155, p. 431.

94. Sacchetti, *Il Trecentonovelle,* novella 155, p. 433. In the following novella, 156 (pp. 443–447), the protagonist is a phony doctor; this is the summary preceding the story: "Messer Dolcibene, in the guise of a doctor in the district of Ferrara, restores to its correct position the hand of a girl that was twisted and dislocated, and this he does by sitting down on it heavily." The dress of a doctor was so characteristic that in novella 42 (p. 116), Sacchetti notes that a certain official was dressed "in a long cloak and with flaps (*batoli*) on the front so that he looked more like a doctor than a cavalier."

95. The sonnet concludes: "It did the devil no good to have with him the ampules of mortal sin that make men weak." The story is narrated at greater length in D. Cavalca, *Volgarizzamento delle Vite de' SS. Padri* (Milan: Silvestri: 1830), pp. 24–25. See further, C. Frugoni, "Altri luoghi," p. 1575.

96. Scarlet robes were worn by those who had graduated from university with a doctorate; cf.

Boccaccio, *Decameron* 8.9 (ed. Branca, p. 984, n. 1). Fur trimming made of vair was a visible badge of the holder of a medical doctorate.

97. Boccaccio, *Decameron* 8.9 (trans. Musa and Bondanella, p. 529).

98. "[Bruno] aveva dipinto nella sala sua la Quaresima e uno agnusdei all'entrar della camera e sopra l'uscio della via uno orinale, acciò che coloro che avessero del suo consiglio bisogno il sapessero riconoscer dagli altri; e in una sua loggetta gli aveva dipinta la battaglia de' topi e delle gatte." Boccaccio, *Decameron* 8.9 (ed. Branca p. 991; trans. Musa and Bondanella, pp. 533–34). Boccaccio normally uses the word *gatta* (female cat; plural *gatte*), as he does here, to refer to cats generically; see Branca's n. 6, p. 697.

99. Boccaccio, *Decameron* 8.9 (trans. Musa and Bondanella, pp. 535 and 540). Gloves and long robes are characteristic features of the dress of doctors.

100. Riché and Alexandre-Bidon, *L'enfance au Moyen Âge*, pp. 45 and 68.

101. Lent as a warrior leading an austere army of fish and battling victoriously against Carnival and his alluring army of choice animal flesh, followed by the triumph of Love, is the subject of a long section (stanzas 1067–1314) of Ruiz, *Book of Good Love*. M. Feo has published a Latin work from the second half of the twelfth century in which "Lent" and "Carnival" exchange letters about which months of the year each will dominate; M. Feo, "Il carnevale dell'umanista," in *Tradizione classica e letteratura umanistica per Alessandro Perosa,* ed. Roberto Cardini et al., 2 vols. (Rome: Bulzoni, 1985), vol. 1, pp. 25–93.

102. Held, with many other works by Brueghel, in the Kunsthistorisches Museum at Vienna.

103. *Phaedri Augusti liberti Fabularum Aesopiarum libri,* 4.6, "Pugna murium et mustelarum." The edition I use is Phaedrus, *Le favole, testo latino a fronte,* Italian translation by Elda Bossi (Bologna: Zanichelli, 1963); 4.6, pp. 168–69. The military leaders of the mice, hampered by the crests they are wearing so that their followers will recognize them, are unable to get away so easily and are eaten by the victorious weasels; the moral of Phaedrus is that in adversity the leaders are always the first to suffer.

104. Naturally the weasel, after devouring the mice, gets into the chicken coop and kills all the chickens, for which the inexorable farm wife condemns it to death. *Esopo toscano dei frati e dei mercanti trecenteschi,* ed. V. Branca (Venice: Marsilio, 1989), fable 40, pp. 182–185.

105. For an edition of the poem of Theodorus Prodromus, with a German translation and an interesting commentary, see Herbert Hunger, *Der byzantinische Katz-Mäuse-Krieg:* (Graz, Vienna, and Cologne: Böhlau, 1968). An excerpt containing the funeral of the mouse Creillo and the account of his death can be found in R. Cantarella, *Poeti bizantini* (Milan: Vita e pensiero, 1948), vol. 2, pp. 826–831.

106. Hunger (who in turn cites E. Weiss, the first to make the connection with Boccaccio's novella), discusses at length the relationship between the *Katomyomachia,* an imitation of the pseudo-Homeric *Batrachomyomachia,* and the fresco at Pürgg. He denies (pp. 68ff.) the hypothesis that the poem was known in Austria on account of the matrimony, in the middle of the twelfth century, between Theodora, the niece of the Byzantine emperor Emanuel Comnenus, and Jasormirgott, the duke of Bamberg. Theodorus Prodromus relates the story of a lone cat attacked by many mice (though other cats appear in the poem, but not as combatants), whereas in the fresco at Pürgg a horde of mice are attacked by a throng of cats. Hunger believes rather that they may both be related to generic motifs and cites several miniatures, in particular one found in an English Book of Hours from the first quarter of the fourteenth century (London, British Library, Harleian MS 6563, fol. 72r), in which a cat defends a tower by hurling stones down on the mice. Apart from the problem of the dates, it seems to me that this miniature would demonstrate exactly the opposite of what Hunger maintains. (It is reproduced in L. M. C. Randall, *Images in the Margins of Gothic Manuscripts* [Berkley and Los Angeles: University of California Press, 1966], fig. 99.) I am most grateful to

Claudio Ciociola for valuable bibliographic help in relation to the battle of mice and the cats. For a reproduction of the fresco at Pürgg, see Otto Demus, *Romanesque Mural Painting* (New York: Abrams, 1970), plate 293 (in the German original, *Romanische Wandmalerei* [1968], and the Italian translation, *Pittura murale romanica* [1969], the illustrations are numbered differently, and this one appears as plate 236).

107. J. Puig y Cadafalch, A. de Folguera, and J. Goday y Casals, *L'arquitectura romànica a Catalunya* (Barcelona: Institut d'Estudios catalans, 1909–1918; 3 vols.), vol. 3, fig. 1072.

108. The oldest surviving print is from 1521. For a catalog of all the printed witnesses and a critical edition of the poem, see M. Chiesa in *Il Parnaso e la zucca: Testi e studi folenghiani,* ed. M. Chiesa and S. Gatti (Alessandria: Edizioni dell'Orso, 1995), pp. 13–51 (with the text of the poem, "La gran battaglia de li gatti e de li sorzi. Cosa nuova bellissima da ridere e da piacere" [The great battle of the cats and the mice. Something new and very fine, for laughter and pleasure] edited by Chiesa on pp. 13–37). At pp. 103–118 ("Un anonimo raffinato per un letteratissimo poemetto popolareggiante"), Chiesa signals the citation from Boccaccio but without drawing any further conclusions; perhaps inadvertently he fails to mention the priority of Hunger, whom he does nevertheless quote, in providing this and many other notices and references.

109. F. V. Essling, *Livres à figures vénitiennes,* 2 vols. (Paris: Olschki-H. Leclerc, 1909), vol. 2, p. 421, no. 2111 and p. 422, no. 2113. In woodcut no. 2111 on p. 421 (= figure 81 in this book) the cat wearing the shield almost looks like a boar.

110. Boccaccio, *Decameron* 8.9 (trans. Musa and Bondanella, p. 532). The doctors often doubled as drug and spice dealers, preparing and selling the medicines they themselves had prescribed; see p. 109.

111. Boccaccio, *Decameron* 8.9 (trans. Musa and Bondanella, p. 533).

112. Boccaccio, *Decameron* 8.9 (translation adapted from Musa and Bondanella, p. 539).

113. Francesco Alunno was the humanistic name of Francesco del Bailo (b. Ferrara, c. 1485, d. circa 1556, Venice); a student of language and a calligrapher, he composed *Ricchezze della lingua volgare sopra il Boccaccio* (1543–51), a glossary of the *Decameron.*

114. Francesco Alunno, cited by V. Branca in his edition of Boccaccio, *Decameron* 8.9 (p. 999, n. 7).

115. Boccaccio, *Decameron* 8.9 (trans. Musa and Bondanella, p. 539). The lavatories or pits were emptied only at night. At Siena the regulation was that "no one should empty out, or have emptied out, pits and lavatories except at night, after the third sounding of the bell of the commune." *Il Costituto del Comune di Siena volgarizzato,* vol. 2, d. V, r. CLX, p. 301, cited in Balestracci and Piccinni, *Siena nel Trecento,* p. 85. But in the more modest houses there were no lavatories, as we can deduce from the novella of Sercambi in which the protagonist, Bertoldo Adimari, "had made his ease" in the same room in which he lay sick. G. Sercambi, *Novelle,* ed. G. Sinicropi, 2 vols. (Bari: Laterza, 1972), vol. 1, novella 24, p. 121.

116. The church of the Monastery of Ripoli in via della Scala was suppressed, but the facade is still there today. At Siena, a rubric of the *Costituto* of 1262 tried to make people respect a few places at least. (d. I, r. CCLXXVI, p. 109: "On not making filth in the piazzas and streets near the churches of the Franciscans and the Dominicans"); Balestracci and Piccinni, *Siena nel Trecento,* p. 86.

117. "But if you only knew the things I used to do with my friends at night in Bologna, when we were out for women, you would be amazed. By God's faith, there was that one night when one of them refused to come with us (she was a skinny little wench, and what's worse, she was no taller than the palm of your hand), but after I gave her a few punches and picked her up off the ground, I think I must have carried her a stone's throw before convincing her to come with us." Boccaccio, *Decameron* 8.9 (trans. Musa and Bondanella, pp. 540–41). For Simone's boast of braving the nighttime cold, see p. 173.

118. "… and when you are mounted firmly on its back, fold your arms across your chest in courtly fashion and never touch the beast again." Boccaccio, *Decameron* 8.9 (trans. Musa and Bondanella, pp. 540–41 for all the passages cited). In other words, Buffalmacco is instructing Simone to keep his arms folded on his breast, a typical gesture denoting polite respect that was often assumed by waiters serving their masters at table. By forbidding the doctor to touch his mount, the painters would keep him from discovering the trick. As well, being unable to steady himself, Simone's discomfort at the rough ride to which Buffalmacco planned to subject him would be greatly increased.

119. In other words, Buffalmacco was wearing his costume with the fur facing out, the way furs are worn today—a habit that betrays ostentation rather than the most rational way to protect oneself against the cold. In the Middle Ages fur garments were normally worn with the fur side facing in toward the wearer's skin, as a warm lining.

120. Boccaccio, *Decameron* 8.9 (trans. Musa and Bondanella, p. 541).

121. This is also the incipit of the French version of the battle between Lent (Caresme) and Carnival (Charnage); cf. *Il Parnaso e la zucca*, p. 13.

122. "Nel tempo che parlava li animali / e che più libertà concessa gli era, anzi che invidia e suoi diversi mali/ venisse a disturbar sua pace intiera, /regnava un re de gotti e de orinali,/ anzi de' gatti, il qual con faccia altera / con mille tordi stato era in battaglia, / ed era imperador de la Gattaglia. Per nome si chiamava re Gattone. . . . Avea Gatton merdifico e potente / diece reami sotto sua corona; / ogniun di lor ne l'arme sì possente / che fuggito seria da ogni persona / e tenuto averebbe a fronte il niente; / tal che pel mondo già la fama suona /de 'sto signor magnanimo e de quelli/ destruzion de sardelle e gambarelli." *La gran battaglia de li gatti e de li sorzi*, strophes 1–3; in *Il Parnaso e la zucca*, pp. 13–14.

123. "He was armored all over with shit / because while fleeing out of a kitchen / he bolted in fear into a sewage pipe / because Donna Catarina was right behind him / who because he had stolen a ham from her / wanted to thrash him with a stick / and he, to escape such a disaster / dropped the ham and gained that coat of armor" ("Armato era costui di merda tutto/ perché, fuggendo fuor de una cucina, / entrò per tema dentro de un condutto / ch'avea a le spalle donna Catarina, / che per averli furato un persutto / li volea co un baston dar disciplina: / ed ello per fuggir tanta sciagura / lassò il persuto e acquistò l'armatura" *La gran battaglia de li gatti e de li sorzi*, strophe 6; in *Il Parnaso e la zucca*, p. 15). The vaunted courage of Simone, when he goes to the lavatory at night, is echoed in the great courage of the emperor Gattone, who was so proud of his ten subordinate kings that "often through overflowing and great delight / he shit in the bed without even noticing" ("spesso per superchio e gran diletto/senza avedersi cacava nel letto" *La gran battaglia de li gatti e de li sorzi*, strophe 16; in *Il Parnaso e la zucca*, p. 19). The whole poem takes place in a heavily flatulent and scatological atmosphere, similar to Buffalmacco's description of "the countess of Civillari" and her followers in Boccaccio's novella. "O how many strong belches, O how many farts / were seen tumbling to the ground one after another! / And how many baskets, which were their helmets / and containers of urine were seen flying through the air" ("O quanti forti rutti, o quanti petti/ si vedeano un su l'altro a terra andare! / e quanti cesti, ch'eran lor elmeti, / ed orinali per l'aria volare!" *La gran battaglia de li gatti e de li sorzi*, strophe 72; in *Il Parnaso e la zucca*, p. 35). And the brave mouse Gratugia, "shrieks and howls and roars and leaps and darts / and in his ire shits square turds" ("E stride, ed urla, e mugia, e salta, e guizza, / e caca stronzi quadri per la stizza"; strophe 24, p. 21).

124. "a caval de ingistare e de mortari . . . ; . . . elmi di pelice; / e sopraveste de dossi e de vari, / e lancie de caligo e fumo e vento/ e d'un 'lassami star!' pien d'ardimento." *La gran battaglia de li gatti e de li sorzi*, strophe 32; in *Il Parnaso e la zucca*, pp. 23–24. *Ingistara* o '*nguistara*, according to the *Vocabolario della Crusca*, a major historical dictionary of the Italian language, is the same thing as a *guastada* (a carafe). For the *guastadetta* (little carafe) of Mazzeo della Montagna of Salerno, see below, p. jj. For the vair, a symbol of a member of the medical profession, see nn. 91 and 96 above.

125. Literally "without being doped" ("senza essere adoppiato"), that is, without having an opium-based anaesthetic administered to him.

126. Boccaccio, *Decameron* 4.10 (trans. Musa and Bondanella, pp. 302–303).

127. Boccaccio, *Decameron* 4.10 (trans. Musa and Bondanella, p. 301).

128. Biblioteca comunale di Città di Castello, *Riformanze*, vol. IX, fol. 75v, 8 June 1374 (emphasis added).

129. Born in around 1156, Bona lived the opposite of a retiring life, maintaining herself with the labor of her own hands by spinning and by curing sprains and dislocations. She traveled widely, completing numerous pilgrimages, including two to Jerusalem, nine to Santiago de Compostela, and many to Rome. When her ailing body prevented her from leaving Pisa anymore, Bona continued to travel "per desiderio" (in her wishes) by traversing space in spirit. See my article "Santa Bona, pellegrina 'per desiderio,'" in *Gli universi del fantastico*, ed. V. Branca and C. Ossola (Florence: Vallecchi, 1988), pp. 259–272.

130. Frugoni, "Santa Bona, pellegrina 'per desiderio,'" p. 272.

131. Beneath every episode of the Franciscan cycle there is a caption, today largely fragmentary. I give the texts of these as they were transcribed and integrated by B. Marinangeli, "La serie di affreschi giotteschi rappresentanti la vita di S. Francesco nella Chiesa Superiore di Assisi," in *Miscellanea Francescana* 13 (1911): pp. 97–112. Marinangeli was in turn able to consult a transcription of the painted words carried out by an unnamed individual in the seventeenth century, when they were already difficult to read. See "Descrizione della Basilica di San Francesco," Assisi, Biblioteca comunale, fondo moderno, MS 148, fols. 1–83. The text of this manuscript is given in Ludovico da Pietralunga, *La Basilica di San Francesco d'Assisi*, with introduction, notes, and commentary by P. Scarpellini (Treviso: Canova, 1982), pp. 121–22. For the correspondence of the frescoes with the text of the *Legenda maior* of San Bonaventura of Bagnoregio, which became the official biography of San Francesco from 1266 on, see "Bonaventurae Legenda maior s. Francisci," in *Legendae S. Francisci Assisensis saeculis XIII et XIV conscriptae*, vol. 10 of *Analecta Franciscana* (Ad Claras Aquas prope Florentiam: Ex Typ. Collegii s. Bonaventurae, 1926–1941), pp. 557–652.

132. "Beatus Franciscus Ioannem de civitate Ilerda, vulneratum ad mortem et a medicis desperatum, et se, dum vulneraretur, devote invocantem, statim perfectissime liberavit, sacris suis manibus ligaturas solvens et plagas suavissime tangens" (= *Leg. maior, De miraculis* I, 5).

133. There are also, however, rolled sheets of paper strung together, candles, and sponges. Notaries too went to the spice dealers to get the supplies they needed. A perpetually absent-minded notary in one of Sacchetti's novellas lost a profitable opportunity because he did not have the instruments he needed to draft a will at hand. "So he planned to stock up with enough ink and sheets of paper and pens and a pen case, so that the same thing would not happen again. And he went to a spice dealer and bought a block of sheets, and wrapping them tightly, put them in his purse. And he bought an ampule with the reservoir full of ink and attached it to his belt. And he bought not just a pen but a bundle of pens and worked hard for a whole day to sharpen a bunch of them, which he slung at his side in a leather satchel for holding spices." Sacchetti, *Il Trecentonovelle*, novella 163, p. 469.

134. Sick people would often make a vow to offer a waxen image of the part of the body that was affected on the tomb of the saint they were invoking, should they be granted a return to health.

135. Sacchetti, *Trecentonovelle*, novella 109, p. 287.

136. *El códice de Florencia*, vol. 1, fol. 112r, vol. 2, pp. 104–105.

137. Boccaccio, *Decameron* 4.1 (adapted from Musa and Bondanella, pp. 252–53).

138. Boccaccio, *Decameron* 4.1 (adapted from Musa and Bondanella, pp. 256–57).

139. Boccaccio, *Decameron* 10.4 (trans. Musa and Bondanella, p. 618).

140. Christine de Pizan, *Epistre d'Othéa,* Paris, Bibl. Nat., MS Fr. 848, fol. 19v., reproduced in C. Frugoni, "The Imagined Woman," ch. 11 in *A History of Women in the West,* vol. 2, *Silences of the Middle Ages,* ed. Christiane Klapisch-Zuber, pp. 336–422, fig. 31, p. 387. Women were given official permission to practice medicine professionally only in exceedingly rare cases, and in even fewer cases were they admitted to universities like Paris to study medicine; see C. Opitz, "Life in the Late Middle Ages," ch. 9 in *A History of Women in the West,* vol. 2, *Silences of the Middle Ages,* pp. 267–317, in particular 297–300.

141. J. C. Schmitt, *The Holy Greyhound: Guinefort, Healer of Children since the Thirteenth Century,* trans. Martin Thom (Cambridge: Cambridge University Press; Paris: Éditions de la maison des sciences de l'homme, 1983), ch. 5, pp. 68–82, translated from *Le saint lévrier: Guinefort, guérisseur d'enfants depuis le XIIIe siècle* (Paris: Flammarion, 1979), see pp. 101–121.

142. According to a fanciful etymology of Pliny (*Natural History* 7.7), Julius Caesar "got his name because he was born from the incised uterus of his mother" ("a caeso matris utero dictus").

143. Boccaccio, *Decameron* 10.4 (trans. Musa and Bondanella, p. 617).

144. Riché and Alexandre-Bidon, *L'enfance au Moyen Âge,* p. 85.

145. There is a close connection between this problem and the spread of the cesarean section, always performed after the death of the pregnant woman, which was obligatory from the end of the twelfth century and was reconfirmed by the Council of Trier in 1310; Riché and Alexandre-Bidon, *L'enfance au Moyen Âge,* p. 87.

146. C. Frugoni, "Le mistiche, le visioni e l'iconografia: Rapporti ed influssi," in *Temi e problemi nella mistica femminile trecentesca,* Convegni del centro di Studi sulla spiritualità medioevale, 20 (Todi: Accademia Tudertina, 1983), pp. 139–144, quotation at p. 28.

CHAPTER FOUR

1. Guillelmi Abbatis S. Theodorici, *De natura corporis et animae, libri duo; PL* 180, col. 715. Guillaume de Saint-Thierry was an author of the twelfth century. The judgment he utters here was influenced by the pessimistic view prevalent in antiquity, according to which babies are born wicked, dominated by their instincts, like the animals. Saint Augustine makes the picture darker still, because he thinks of the newborn baby as a sinner, the heir of the sin committed by humanity's first parents. Riché and Alexandre-Bidon, *L'enfance au Moyen Âge,* p. 22.

2. "Beati qui crediderunt et non viderunt" (John 20:29). This sermon expands to include a discussion of life's other little matters, all of which are seen from a vigorously mercantile standpoint; even sleep is a loss, since "it takes away half your time; for as long as you are asleep, you can't accomplish anything." Giordano da Pisa, sermon 10 for 21 December 1304 in Santa Reparata; da Pisa, *Prediche del 1304,* p. 46.

3. Sacchetti, *Il Trecentonovelle,* novella 115, p. 300.

4. See the documentation gathered in Balestracci and Piccinni, *Siena nel Trecento,* p. 60. At Siena the authorities attempted to isolate prostitutes and malefactors by making it illegal to rent houses to them. The existence of brothels managed by the city itself was however benignly accepted, and the authorities shifted the one located directly behind the Palazzo Pubblico, which "the young men won't go to because they are ashamed to be seen" (p. 61), to a more secluded spot.

5. From the statute of the road supervisors, I, cc. 4–5, cited by Balestracci and Piccinni, *Siena nel Trecento,* p. 83.

6. *Il Costituto di Siena volgarizzato,* vol. 2, d. III, r. CCLII, p. 111, cited in Balestracci and Piccinni, *Siena nel Trecento,* p. 92.

7. When we observe a row of holes in the walls of a medieval house today, in Siena for example,

we must not forget to restore, in our mind's eye, the lost overhang, for that house once resembled the ones painted by Simone in fig. 98. But these mental restorations also have to be done with care, because such holes might have served to anchor not the struts supporting an overhang, but the scaffolding at the time of construction. In the latter case, when the house was finished these "scaffold holes" (*buche pontaie*) were not filled in, because they might be needed again in the future. In the middle ages scaffolding was never erected from the ground up; it was always suspended above ground, and so they needed to be able to attach it firmly to the surface of the wall.

8. *Le mesnagier de Paris,* 1.75, pp. 302–303.

9. Riché and Alexandre-Bidon, *L'enfance au Moyen Âge,* p. 85.

10. Riché and Alexandre-Bidon, *L'enfance au Moyen Âge,* p. 38. Note as well this account of a miracle of Santa Francesca Romana (1384–1440): "A child had died, suffocated during the night at its mother's side; the mother appealed, in tears, to the blessed Francesca, who was moved to compassion; she prayed, and then touched him, and he was immediately resuscitated." The text comes from a subtitle under a fresco depicting this miracle, part of a cycle of frescoes illustrating her miracles painted by Antoniazzo Romano in 1468, in the monastery where the holy woman had founded a community of religious women, the Oblates of Maria; it is today the Monastery of the Oblates of Santa Francesca Romana at Tor de' Specchi. See G. Brizzi, "Contributo all'iconografia di Francesca Romana" in *Una santa tutta romana: Saggi e ricerche nel VI centenario della nascita di Francesca Bussa dei Ponziani, 1384–1984* (Monte Oliveto Maggiore [Siena]: L'Ulivo, 1984), p. 286.

11. Here are some queries which Burchard suggests confessors put: "Did you smother your infant involuntarily, or suffocate him under the weight of your clothing, and this after baptism had been performed?" "Did you find your infant beside you, smothered, when you and your husband were lying in bed together, and it was not clear whether it had been suffocated by the father or by you, or had died a natural death?" Burchardi, *Decretorum liber decimus nonus, De poenitentia, PL* 140, cols. 951–976, here at col. 975.

12. "Considering that she did not have sufficient milk to nourish both girls, she [the mother] decided to hand one daughter [Catherine's twin, Giovanna] over to another nurse, and keep the other [Catherine] at home to be nursed with her own milk." But Giovanna, shortly after being baptized, "flew to heaven." The mother stated that she had given birth to twenty-five children, and that she had not suckled any of them except for Catherine; the reason she gave was that, exceptionally, she did not become pregnant again until after Catherine's breast feeding was complete. *Vita s. Catherinae Senensis, AA. SS. Aprilis, III* (Antwerp: apud M. Cnobarum, 1675), p. 860.

13. Riché and Alexandre-Bidon, *L'enfance au Moyen Âge,* p. 63.

14. These calculations apply to Tuscany; Riché and Alexandre-Bidon, *L'enfance au Moyen Âge,* p. 58.

15. Riché and Alexandre-Bidon, *L'enfance au Moyen Âge,* p. 68.

16. See fig. 113.

17. Discussed in Riché and Alexandre-Bidon, *L'enfance au Moyen Âge,* p. 79.

18. In the detail shown in fig. 107, we see the Baby Jesus with his top beside him and his mother keeping an eye on him. She is working with four knitting needles to prepare the "seamless tunic" described in John 19:23 for her Son. Having her work with four needles is a brilliant way to justify pictorially this detail from John's gospel.

19. Jean Froissart, *L'Espinette amoureuse,* ed. A. Fourrier (Paris: Klincksieck, 1972), pp. 53–55.

20. "Straightaway living blood and water flowed from the side of the Crucified into his face and the frontal part of his cloak as he was praying, the way boys like to make water spurt through a reed." *AA. SS. Augusti, IV* (Antwerp: 1739), pp. 719–737, p. 732.

21. Longinus is the blind centurion from the apocryphal Acts of Pilate; he regained his sight

when he was touched by the blood and the water that he himself had caused to flow with a blow of his spear to Christ's side.

22.   Riché and Alexandre-Bidon, *L'enfance au Moyen Âge,* p. 13.

23.   The device is reproduced in Riché and Alexandre-Bidon, *L'enfance au Moyen Âge,* p. 69.

24.   He lived in the twelfth century in England; according to the legend, he died at the age of twelve, murdered by the Jews. *De s. Willelmo puero martire, AA. SS.,* Martii, III, (Antwerp, 1668), p. 590: "Finally he was given over to a certain fur merchant in Norwich, to be instructed in that trade."

25.   Riché and Alexandre-Bidon, *L'enfance au Moyen Âge,* p. 162.

26.   In the countryside, children accompanied their parents at work in the fields, and brought flocks of sheep and herds of pigs to pasture. Pietro de' Crescenzi advises giving them the task of continually making scarecrows move and agitating rods with little bells attached, to keep birds away. Pietro de' Crescenzi, *Livre des profits champêtres,* copy in the Bibliothèque Nationale, Paris, Réserve des livres rares et précieux, 19, p. 30, cited by Riché and Alexandre-Bidon, *L'enfance au Moyen Âge,* p. 167. *Livre des profits champêtres* is the title of the French translation of the celebrated work *Liber ruralium commodorum,* written by Pietro de' Crescenzi in 1305.

27.   Riché and Alexandre-Bidon, *L'enfance au Moyen Âge,* p. 171.

28.   Boccaccio, *Decameron* 5.7 (trans. Musa and Bondanella, p. 352).

29.   P. Torriti, *La Pinacoteca nazionale di Siena: I dipinti dal XII al XV secolo* (Genoa: Sagep, 1977), pp. 228–9 and figs. 269–70. The altarpiece has the Madonna and Child at the center, enthroned and surrounded by angels and Saints Peter, Paul, Nicholas, and John the Baptist. In the wing on the left, the Nativity; in the one on the right, the Crucifixion. These subjects are the customary ones, those believed best suited to act as the focus of prayer in the home. Altar pieces of reduced dimensions begin to appear as ornaments in private houses, especially in the bedrooms, in the fourteenth century.

30.   In medieval Latin literature the Arabs are called "Saracens," a word falsely etymologized as meaning "descendants of Sarah." Later this was corrected to "Agareni" or "descendants of Hagar," since Ishmael, who was held to be the progenitor of the Arabs, was begotten by Abraham and the slave Hagar, not Abraham and his wife Sarah. The story of Adeodato is recounted in the *Legenda aurea* of Iacopo da Varazze in two different versions: in the first Adeodato is a boy, in the second a young man originally from Normandy. Da Varazze, *Legenda aurea,* ch. 3, pp. 22–29, on p. 29.

31.   The boy was called Adeodato (in Latin, Adeodatus) because his father, who was devoted to that saint, believed that God had given him a son after Nicholas had interceded. The father had also built a chapel in honor of Saint Nicholas, and celebrated his feast day every year.

32.   The room of the parents is tilted forward slightly in comparison to that of the pagan king, and the child offers himself not just to the arms of his parents, but to us as well, meeting our gaze in the foreground.

33.   Da Varazze, *Legenda aurea,* ch. 3, p. 28.

CHAPTER FIVE

1.   Boccaccio, *Decameron* 8.9 (adapted from Musa and Bondanella, pp. 537–38).

2.   A little jewel of the fourteenth century, shaped like a shield, was certainly intended for a French child, for it bears the words "A, B, C, c'est ma leçon." It is part of the collection of the Victoria and Albert Museum of London; Riché and Alexandre-Bidon, *L'enfance au Moyen Âge,* pp. 140–141, fig. at p. 140.

3.   G. Dalli Regoli, *Il maestro di Borsigliana: Un pittore del '400 in Alta Val di Serchio* (Lucca: Pacini-Fazzi, 1987). Numerous examples of panels of this type are assembled in D. Alexandre-Bidon, "La lettre volée: Apprendre à lire à l'enfant au Moyen Age," *Annales* 44, no. 2 (July–Aug. 1989): 953–992.

4. "Audi, filia, et vide, et inclina aurem tuam,/ et obliviscere populum tuum et domum patris tui / et concupiscet rex decorem tuum / quoniam ipse est Dominus Deus tuus." Psalm 44:11–12 in the Vulgate, 45:11–12 in other textual traditions of the bible. [TRANSLATOR'S NOTE: the Latin text, which the translation into English reflects, is that of the Vulgate in its traditional form, but the modern critical text of the Vulgate treats the word *Deus* as an interpolation and modern scholarship interprets this psalm as a royal wedding song. For obvious reasons, C. Frugoni quotes the Latin text in the form known to the Middle Ages and interprets the meaning it had for people then.] The miniature is reproduced in C. Frugoni, "The Imagined Woman," fig. 41, p. 399.

5. Psalm 24 in the Vulgate, Psalm 25 in other traditions. In the Hebrew text the initial letters of the lines of this psalm form an acrostic, producing all the letters of the alphabet in order.

6. Held in the Musées royaux des Beaux-Arts in Brussels. According to a legendary tradition, Saint Anna married three times. By her first husband, Joachim, she had Mary, who in turn gave birth to Jesus. By her second husband, Clopas, she had Mary Clopas, the wife of Alpheus. This couple in turn begot James the Less, the future apostle, Joseph the Just, Simon, and Jude. Saint Anna was supposed to have married a third time with Salomé, by whom she had Mary Salomé, the wife of Zebedee. This couple begot James the Greater, the future apostle, and John, the future evangelist.

7. The parents of Saint Gérard of Aurillac (end of the ninth century) had him learn to read from the Psalter, as did those of San Bardo (eleventh century), who was entrusted to an old woman "with a Psalter so she could teach him to read." Hildegard of Bingen (twelfth century) professed herself ignorant, because, "as the daughters of nobles do," she had ended her studies with the Psalter. Riché and Alexandre-Bidon, *L'enfance au Moyen Âge,* p. 141.

8. An affirmation of the theologian and philosopher Jean de Gerson at the end of the fourteenth century, in his *ABC des simples gens,* vol. 7 in *Oeuvres complètes* (Paris, 1986), p. 154, cited in Riché and Alexandre-Bidon, *L'enfance au Moyen Âge,* p. 192.

9. It is the "Krumauer Bilder codex," so-called from the name of the convent of Friars Minor from which it comes, and held at the Österreichische Nationalbibliothek of Vienna (MS 370). The facsimile is edited by G. Schmidt, with transcription and German translation by F. Unterkircher (Graz: Verlagsanstalt Graz, 1967).

10. "Hic puella post quinque annos instruitur alfabetum et post hec psalterium."

11. "Dum laveretur puella, invenerunt auereas literas in pectore scriptas: 'diligo te sicut cor meum.'" Fol. 132v, Krumauer Bilder codex, p. 120.

12. The stylus is a little wand used for writing on waxed tablets: it is sharpened at one end, to make letters in the wax, and flattened at the other, to scrape or smooth over the wax. [The luck and sagacity of a young scholar, Laura Lametti, have brought to light, from a chest of papers in a private residence, a notebook containing text and drawings made by Lodovico Castellini, a scholar who between 1770 and 1780 described and recorded the details he had found most striking in Palazzo Trinci. In this notebook she found transcripts of two receipts for payments made in 1411 and 1412, the originals of which Castellini had had before him, from which it results that the painter who, no doubt with the help of a group of assistants, made the frescos in the Sala degli imperatori, the Camera delle rose, and the Loggia, is without any doubt Gentile da Fabriano. This valuable discovery will draw much attention because on one hand it undermines a lengthy list of attributions, and on the other makes it necessary to rethink the entire artistic biography of Gentile.]

13. The scene is illustrated in a miniature from a Pseudo-Matthew of the thirteenth century, held at the Bibliothèque Nationale, Paris, MS Lat. 2688, fol. 36v, and reproduced in Riché and Alexandre-Bidon, *L'enfance au Moyen Âge,* p. 130.

14. Boccaccio, *Decameron* 4.1 (adapted from Musa and Bondanella, p. 254).

15. Guiberti abbatis Novigensis, *De vita sua,* ed. E. Labande (Paris: Les Belles Lettres, 1981), 1.6, pp. 38–41.

16. See the introduction above, p. 12.

17. The miniature, from a ninth-century copy of the *Peristephanon* of Prudentius (Bern, Bürger-bibliothek, MS 264b, fols. 60v–61r), is reproduced in Riché and Alexandre-Bidon, *L'enfance au Moyen Âge*, p. 206.

18. P. Riché, *Ecoles et enseignement dans le haut Moyen Âge* (Paris: 1989), p. 244.

19. In my school days, the story featured a wolf, a cabbage, and a goat.

20. Hugonis de Sancto Victore, *Euditionis didascalicae*, 6.3, PL 176, col. 799.

Chapter Six

1. Not all women working as spinners were necessarily illiterate. The wife of one wool worker was perfectly capable of reading, since she asked her abusive husband to put his orders "in writing" for her. This woman "awoke every morning in winter to rise and spin the finely carded wool on the spinning machine," disturbing the sleep of the painter Buffalmacco (here called Buonamico), who at that hour was going to bed after having spent the whole night painting. There was only a thin partition of brick between the painter's room and that of the woman, and the noise of the wheels of the spinning machine bothered him. Through a clever ruse the artist succeeded in getting the husband to stop demanding so much labor from his poor wife. Sacchetti, *Il Trecentonovelle*, novella 192, pp. 568–573.

2. Boccaccio, *Decameron* preface (Musa and Bondanella, pp. 2–3).

3. Giordano da Pisa, *Quaresimale fiorentino, 1305–1306*, ed. C. Delcorno (Florence: Sansoni, 1974), p. 75. At this point in the transcript a comment has been inserted: "And the reader said, 'I saw the person who first invented it and made it, and I spoke to him" (E disse il lettore: 'Io vidi colui che prima la trovò e fece, e favellaigli.)

4. Boccaccio, *Decameron* 5.10 (adapted from Musa and Bondanella, pp. 370–72).

Chapter Seven

1. To make tinder, the "householder of Paris" advises taking rotted nutshells, boiling them with lye for two days and a night, adding urine at the end, and finally rinsing them thoroughly in clean water. After that they have to be dried very slowly; once dry, they are to be pounded with a mallet until they acquire the appearance of a sponge. To light a fire with flint and steel, you have to use a quantity of this tinder equal in size to a large pea; for lighting candles, it is better to impregnate the tinder with sulphur. *Le mesnagier de Paris*, 2.5.348, pp. 794–795.

2. In the darkness of the palace of the Longobard king Agilulfo, the enamored groom makes his way at night to the queen's bedroom: "He lighted his torch by striking light with the flint and steel he brought with him for this purpose and, wrapping himself up in the cloak, made his way to the door of the bedroom." Boccaccio, *Decameron* 3.2 (Musa and Bondanella, p. 173).

3. The unhappy Ghismunda, to let her lover know her plans, "wrote him a letter, and in it she told him what he had to do the following day in order to be with her; then she put it in the hollow of a reed, and, as if in jest, she have it to Guiscardo, saying, 'Make a *soffione* ["blower" or "blowing tube"] of this tonight for your serving girl to keep the fire burning.'" Boccaccio, *Decameron* 4.1 (adapted from Musa and Bondanella, p. 251).

4. See above, p. 155, and chapter 6, n. 4.

5. The *Twelve Proverbs* were each painted on a wooden panel and were subsequently joined together to form a single composition, now in the Museum Mayer van den Bergh in Antwerp. The painter repeated the same figure, but without the inscriptions, in the panel *Netherlandish Proverbs*, painted the following year. Approximately 123 proverbs compose this swarming work of 1559, held in the Staatliche Museen of Berlin.

6. *Le mesnagier de Paris,* 2.3.18, pp. 458–59.

7. Wood was used for the beams and planks of the ceilings, the framework of the roof, the flooring, and the stairs.

8. G. Sercambi, *Novelle,* vol. 1, novella 10, p. 59, cited in Balestracci and Piccinni, *Siena nel Trecento,* p. 165.

9. Agnolo di Tura del Grasso, *Cronaca senese, RIS,* 15.6, fasc. 5, p. 381, records this happening in the year 1320: "There was great celebration, with bonfires, in many places in Siena, and on top of many towers; and in the evening the wind blew strongly, and fire took hold on top of the tower of the Bandinelli, and a number in other towers, and on top of the tower of the Orsa, the one, that is, next to the tower of the Mignanelli, which is called the Torione; and it spread among the bells of the commune, and burned the framework supporting the bells, causing them to fall to the ground inside the tower, and they were broken and wrecked . . ." Paolo di Tommaso Montauri, *Cronaca senese, RIS,* 15.6, fasc. 8, p. 741, has this entry for 1391: "Great celebration, with noise and bells and dancing, and in the evening fires and bonfires on towers and bell towers"; this time, however, they did not get out of control.

10. Balestracci and Piccinni, *Siena nel Trecento,* p. 166, n. 8.

11. *Il Costituto del Comune di Siena volgarizzato,* vol. 2, d. 5, r. 373, p. 392, cited by Balestracci and Piccinni, *Siena nel Trecento,* p. 164.

12. Paolo di Tommaso Montauri, *Cronaca senese, RIS,* 15.6, fasc. 8, p. 774, cited by Balestracci and Piccinni, *Siena nel Trecento,* p. 168. Throughout the year 1347, fire broke out in Florence at frequent intervals; one of the most serious was caused, once again, by the activity of wool workers: "And then on 8 August, a fire started in the parish (*popolo*) of San Martino, close by Orsanmichele, in the shops of wool workers. It started in some heated cloth because of the grease and the excessive heat, and there were 18 houses, shops, and warehouses of wool workers burned, causing very great losses through the burning of cloth and wool and other tools and equipment, not to mention the damage to the houses. And this revealed the influence of the planet Mars, and the sun, and Mercury, considered to have influence in part on our city of Florence, having been in the house of the Lion; or rather the careless guard kept on the fire by those who were supposed to watch it." Villani, *Nuova cronica,* 13.32, vol. 3, p. 376. In another similar passage, in which the chronicler recounts very serious outbreaks of fire throughout the year 1332 (houses and towers collapsed, people died), he once again allows his solid common sense to surface: the fires were indeed propagated by the conjunction of the stars but also by "lack of foresight and care; and on this we ought to place more emphasis." Fires did not just cause material loss: "A fire never takes hold without the whole city becoming agitated, and everyone arming themselves and being very tense." Villani, *Nuova cronica,* 9.207, vol. 2, pp. 771–72.

13. This martyr was roasted to death on a grate.

14. Boccaccio, *Decameron* 6.10 (Musa and Bondanella, p. 409).

15. Sacchetti, *Il Trecentonovelle,* novella 34, p. 91.

16. E. Cecchi, "Le scritte murali," in *Palazzo Davanzati,* ed. M. F. Todorow (Florence: Becocci, 1979), pp. 58–62, at p. 62.

17. Boccaccio, *Decameron,* introduction to day nine (adapted from Musa and Bondanella, p. 558).

18. *Il museo di Palazzo Davanzati a Firenze,* ed. L. Berti (Milan: Electa, n.d), p. 11.

19. Archivio di Stato di Siena, *Consiglio generale,* 204, c. 130, for 10 September 1410, cited in Balestracci and Piccinni, *Siena nel Trecento,* p. 91.

20. Balestracci and Piccinni, *Siena nel Trecento,* p. 147.

21. *Le mesnagier de Paris,* ed. Brereton, 1.7.1, pp. 296–297.

22. *El códice de Florencia de las Cantigas de Alfonso X,* vol. 1, p. 28; vol. 2, fol. 7r. The luxuriant enclosed garden of orange trees and cedars described by Boccaccio in the introduction to the third day appears

to be rather closely modeled on a tapestry, with its thick dark grass abounding in flowers, rabbits, and deer, its arbors of flowering vines, roses, and jasmine, and a marvelous spouting fountain at the center. It is this fountain that endows it with its greatest appeal: the jets of water, the freshness, the rivulets and channels in the meadow, all flowing together finally in a brook that turns two mills further downstream. Around the fountain the young people dine, sing, and dance and are so taken with the beauty of the place that they forgo their afternoon rest and remain, "some reading romances, others playing chess or dice games while the rest slept." And it is when they have gathered around the fountain once again that they begin the stories for that day, after having bathed their faces in the fresh water. Boccaccio, *Decameron,* introduction to day three (Musa and Bondanella, pp. 163–165).

23. Boccaccio, *Decameron,* conclusion to day six (Musa and Bondanella, p. 413).

24. Boccaccio, *Decameron,* conclusion to day two (Musa and Bondanella, p. 160).

25. The astute servant of King Agilulfo does go into the bedroom of the queen but not without taking due precautions: "Having thoroughly washed himself in a hot bath so that the odor of horse manure might not offend the Queen or cause her to suspect a trick." Boccaccio, *Decameron* 3.2 (Musa and Bondanella, pp. 172–73).

26. Riché and Alexandre-Bidon, *L'enfance au Moyen Âge,* p. 63.

27. Boccaccio, *Decameron* 2.2 (Musa and Bondanella, pp. 70–72).

28. In this miniature the draftsman, to illustrate the idea that the water is the right temperature, shows three nude women who have just placed their clothing and underclothing on the pole overhead. One is already in the tub and is helping her friend, who is climbing up on a stool, to enter; the third waits her turn.

29. Boccaccio, *Decameron* 3.6.

30. Boccaccio, *Decameron* 8.10 (Musa and Bondanella, p. 546).

31. Called, in Boccaccio's Italian, "acqua nanfa."

32. Boccaccio, *Decameron* 8.10 (Musa and Bondanella, pp. 546–47).

33. These poles (*stanghe*) filled the role of modern closets, as we have seen.

34. Boccaccio, *Decameron* 8.10 (adapted from Musa and Bondanella, pp. 547–548).

35. Boccaccio, *Decameron* 2.5 (adapted from Musa and Bondanella, pp. 87–88).

36. Boccaccio, *Decameron* 2.5 (trans. Musa and Bondanella, p. 91).

37. Villani, *Nuova Cronica,* 2.1, vol. 1, pp. 60–61.

38. Anonymi Ticinensis (Opicino de Canistris) *Liber de laudibus civitatis Ticinensis,* p. 20. For the pigs of Saint Anthony, see above ch. 3, n. 43.

39. Boccaccio, *Decameron* 8.9 (trans. Musa and Bondanella, p. 541).

40. *Le mesnagier de Paris,* ed. Brereton, 1.9.4–8, pp. 403–407.

41. Boccaccio, *Decameron* 3.2 (trans. Musa and Bondanella, p. 174).

42. "At the crow of the cock, hope returns" (Gallo canente spes redit") runs a verse (taken from the *Aeterne rerum conditor* of Saint Ambrose) written around the figure of a cock carved on the thirteenth-century capital of the eighth column on the left-hand side of the Cathedral of Todi. Grondona, *Todi, storica ed artistica,* p. 108.

Anonymus Ticinensis (Opicinus de Canistris; Opicino de Canistris). *Liber de laudibus civitatis Ticinensis. RIS* II.I.

Baebler, J. J. *Beiträge zu einer Geschichte der lateinischen Grammatik im Mittelalter.* Halle a. S.: Buchhandlung des Waisenhauses, 1885.

Balestracci, D., and G. Piccinni. *Siena nel Trecento: Assetto urbano e strutture edilizie.* Siena: Clusf, 1977.

Bernardino da Siena. *Le prediche volgari.* Vol. I. Ed. C. Cannarozzi. Pistoia: Pacinotti, 1934.

Boccaccio, Giovanni. *Decameron.* Ed. V. Branca. 2 vols. Turin: Einaudi, 1993.

———. *The Decameron.* Trans. Mark Musa and Peter Bondanella. New York and London: W. W. Norton, 1982.

Braunfels, W. *Mittelalterliche Stadtbaukunst in der Toskana.* Berlin: G. Mann, 1959.

Durandus, Gulielmus. *Rationale divinorum officiorum.* Venice: apud Cominum de Tridino, 1572.

El códice de Florencia de las Cantigas de Alfonso X el Sabio. 2 vols. Madrid: Edilán, 1989–1991.

"Frammenti di statuti di Città di Castello, 1261–1273." Ed. G. Magherini-Graziani. *Bollettino di Storia Patria per l'Umbria* 15 (1909): 3–107.

Frandon, V. "Iconographie des saisons dans l'Occident médiéval." *Revue de la B[iblio-thèque] N[ationale]* 50 (winter 1993): 2–8.

Frugoni, C. "Altri luoghi, cercando il paradiso (il ciclo di Buffalmacco nel Camposanto di Pisa e la committenza domenicana)." (1988). *Annali della Scuola Normale Superiore di Pisa,* series 3, 18, no. 4 (1990): 1557–1643.

———. *A Distant City: Images of Urban Experience in the Medieval World.* Trans. W. McCuaig. Princeton: Princeton University Press, 1991.

———. "La rappresentazione dei giullari nelle chiese fino al XII sec." In *Il Contributo dei giullari alla drammaturgia italiana delle origini, Atti del II Convegno di Studio, Viterbo, 17–19 giugno '77,* pp. 113–134. Rome: Bulzoni, 1978.

———. "The Imagined Woman." Ch. 11 of *Silences of the Middle Ages,* ed. Klapisch-Zuber, pp. 336–422. Cambridge, Mass.: Belknap Press of Harvard University Press, 1992.

———. "Santa Bona, pellegrina 'per desiderio.'" In *Gli universi del fantastico.* Ed. V. Branca and C. Ossola, pp. 259–272. Florence: Vallecchi, 1988.

Gioco e giustizia nell'Italia di Comune. Ed. G. Ortalli. Treviso and Rome: Benetton-Viella, 1993.

Giordano da Pisa. *Prediche del B. Giordano da Rivalto dell'ordine de' Predicatori (del 1304, dell'Avvento e della Quaresima).* Ed. M. D. Manni. Florence: G. Viviani, 1739.

Giordano da Pisa. *Prediche inedite del B. Giordano da Rivalto dell'ordine de' Predicatori recitate in Firenze dal 1302 al 1305.* Ed. E. Narducci. Bologna: G. Romagnoli, 1867.

Grondona, C. *Todi: Storica ed artistica.* With additions by M. Grondona. Todi: Pro Todi Editrice, 1993.

Iacopo da Varazze [Iacopo da Varagine; Jacobus a Voragine]. *Legenda aurea.* Ed. Th. Graesse. Osnabrück: Zeller, 1969; photoreprint of the 1890 edition.

Il museo di Palazzo Davanzati a Firenze. Ed. L. Berti. Milan: Electa, n.d.

Il Parnaso e la zucca: Testi e studi folenghiani. Ed. M. Chiesa and S. Gatti. Alessandria: Edizioni dell'Orso, 1995.

Le mesnagier de Paris. Ed. G. E. Brereton. Paris: Le Livre de Poche, 1994.

Liber statutorum Civitatis Castelli. Città di Castello: Antonio Mazzocchi and Nicola and Bartolomeo Gucci, 1538.

Montauri, Paolo di Tommaso. *Cronaca senese conosciuta sotto il nome di Paolo di Tommaso Montauri. RIS* 15.6, fasc. 8, pp. 179–252, 689–835.

Palazzo Davanzati. Ed. M. F. Todorow. Florence: Becocci, 1979.

Palazzo Pubblico di Siena. Vicende costruttive e decorazione. Ed. C. Brandi. Siena: Monte dei Paschi di Siena, 1983.

Pinto, G. *Il libro del Biadaiolo: Carestie e annona a Fireze dalla metà del '200 al 1348.* Florence: Olschki, 1978.

Porci e porcari nel Medioevo, paesaggio, economia, alimentazione. Ed. M. Baruzzi and M. Montanari. Bologna: Clueb, 1981.

Riché, P., and D. Alexandre-Bidon. *L'enfance au Moyen Age.* Paris: Seuil, 1994.

Rigaux, D. "Usages apotropaïques de la fresque dans l'Italie du Nord au XIVe siècle." In *Nicée II, 787–198:Douze siècles d'images religieuses.* Ed. F. Boesflug and N. Lossky, pp. 317–331. Paris: Éditions du Cerf, 1987.

Rizzi, A. *Ludus/ludere: Giocare in Italia alla fine del Medioevo.* Rome: Viella, 1995.

Ruiz, Juan. *The Book of Good Love.* Trans. Elizabeth Drayson Macdonald. London: J. M. Dent, 1999.

Sacchetti, Franco. *Il Trecentonovelle.* Ed. E. Faccioli. Turin: Einaudi, 1970.

Sercambi, G. *Novelle.* Ed. G. Sinicropi. 2 vols. Scrittori d'Italia, 250–251. Bari: Laterza, 1972.

Silences of the Middle Ages. Ed. C. Klapisch-Zuber. Vol. 2 of *A History of Women in the West.* Ed. G. Duby and M. Perrot. Cambridge, Mass.: Belknap Press of Harvard University Press, 1992.

Stefani, Marchionne di Coppo. *Cronaca fiorentina. RIS* 30.1.

Villani, Giovanni. *Nuova cronica.* Ed. G. Porta. 3 vols. Fondazione P. Bembo; Parma: U. Guanda, 1990–1991.

Zdekauer, L. *La vita pubblica dei Senesi nel Dugento.* Siena: L. Lazzeri, 1897.